I0572530
Reader's House
Italian Roots, Canadian Stories
BARBARA AVON
Telling Stories That Haunt, Heal and Inspire Across Genres
INTERVIEW
Voices of Literary Excellence
Insights from Today's Celebrated Authors
EDITOR'S CHOICE
Best Books to Dive Into
available in print
READER'S HOUSE

# Editor's Picks

## Gigglet

### *A.M. BERKOWITZ*

*Heartwarming tale with vibrant illustrations, delightful characters, and valuable lessons on friendship, teamwork, and nature's joys. Perfect children's book!*

Kindle: £6.53

https://bit.ly/4kufCJA

## Caged

### *CC ROB NSON*

A gripping, fast-paced dystopian sequel with high stakes, compelling characters, and relentless tension—Caged keeps readers hooked from start to finish.

Kindle: £3.89

https://tinyurl.com/yeyta4jj

## Delicious Surrender

### *LUCE SUTHERLAND*

Intensely passionate, thrillingly suspenseful, and irresistibly steamy—Delicious Surrender delivers fiery chemistry, gripping tension, and a deeply satisfying romance.

Paperback: £13.99

https://tinyurl.com/mtty5fej

## Henchmen

### *MATTHEW HUGHES*

A gripping, witty fantasy adventure with rich world-building, engaging characters, and masterful storytelling—Hughes delivers intrigue, action, and unforgettable magic.

Paperback: £16.13

https://tinyurl.com/2wbe6ewn

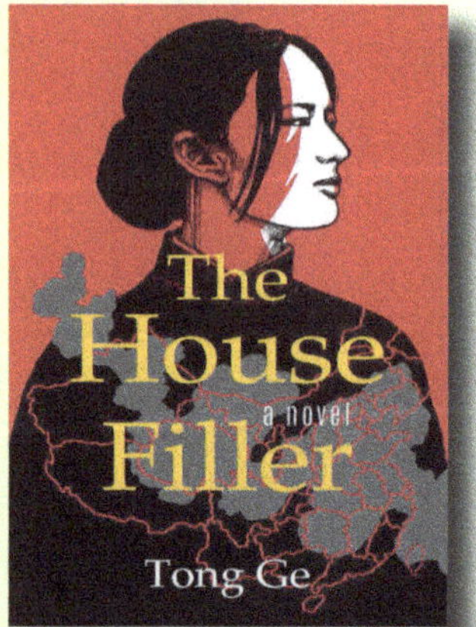


## The House Filler

### *TONG GE*

A beautifully written, emotionally powerful novel that captures resilience, love, and survival amidst the turmoil of war and political unrest.

Paperback: £19.83

https://tinyurl.com/t2n5by5t

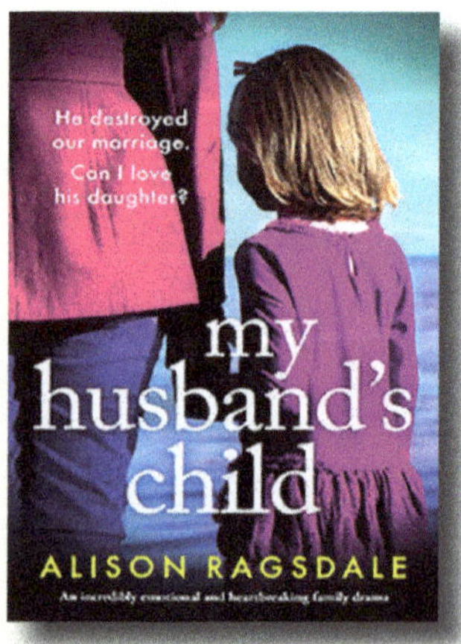


## My Husband's Child

### *ALISON RAGSDALE*

A beautifully written, emotionally gripping novel with vivid characters, heartfelt storytelling, and a captivating exploration of motherhood and sacrifice.

Paperback: £8.99

https://tinyurl.com/4smyyh37

## Wishes Are Free

### *DIANA MERCEDES HOWELL*

A masterfully crafted tale that touches hearts, teaches empathy, and reminds us that friendship comes in unexpected, beautiful forms.

Kindle: £4.61

https://tinyurl.com/3rjenfmz

## Her Eyes Were on the Stars

### *JENNIFER SOMMER*

A masterfully crafted biography that inspires while educating, bringing to life the remarkable legacy of a pioneering female scientist.

Audiobook: £0.99

https://tinyurl.com/4uh9v4sx

# *Your Gateway to Endless Stories*

### Broken Pencil

***J.R. RICE***

A raw, unflinching masterpiece that captures youth's struggles with stunning clarity and emotional depth. Simply unforgettable.

Paperback: £2.35

https://tinyurl.com/z5he4db3

### The Matrix Opal

***STELLA ATRIUM***

A richly imaginative and deeply philosophical fantasy tale, The Matrix Opal enchants with layered characters, poetic interludes, and gripping intrigue.

Paperback: £12.95

https://tinyurl.com/y9rkzwbd

### Lion of the Sky

***RITU HEMNANI***

A beautifully written, emotionally resonant story of friendship, resilience, and hope during one of history's most heartbreaking upheavals.

Paperback: £16.63

https://tinyurl.com/mr2jnxd6

### Seasonal Self-Care Rituals

***SUSAN WE S-BOHLEN***

A beautifully balanced guide blending ancient wisdom with modern living, this book empowers holistic health through mindful, seasonal self-care rituals.

Kindle: £11.99

https://tinyurl.com/z8w3aej9

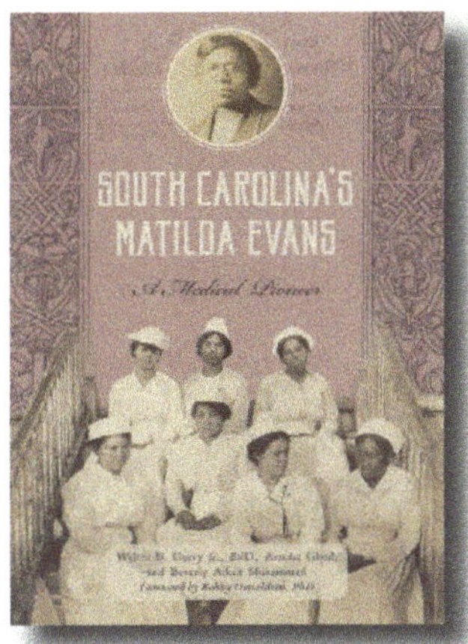


### South Carolina's Matilda Evans

***DR. WALTER B. CURRY JR.***

Insightful, inspiring, and deeply practical—Success is a Choice offers a transformative perspective on personal growth and professional success.

Paperback: £19.09

https://tinyurl.com/2frmhu7m

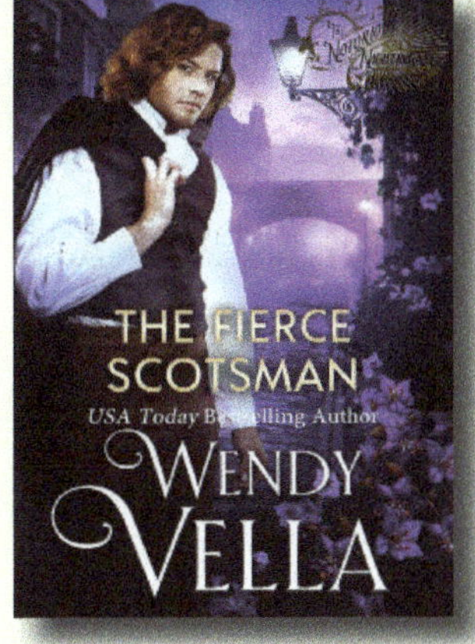


### The Fierce Scotsman

***WENDY VELLA***

A thrilling blend of romance and mystery, The Fierce Scotsman captivates with bold characters, emotional depth, and irresistible chemistry.

Kindle: £4.99

https://tinyurl.com/3djz9p3p

### Ice Cap

***JOAN EPP***

Ice Cap is a charming, heartwarming story with delightful illustrations, spreading kindness, joy, and winter magic for children.

Kindle: £4.05

https://tinyurl.com/42myt2dm

### The Legend of Atlantis and The Science of Geology

***JOSEPH O'DONOGHUE***

An intellectually stimulating exploration, blending geology and mythology, offering fresh insights into the Atlantis legend with a balanced, open-minded approach.

Paperback: £20.44

https://tinyurl.com/jcdyw6by

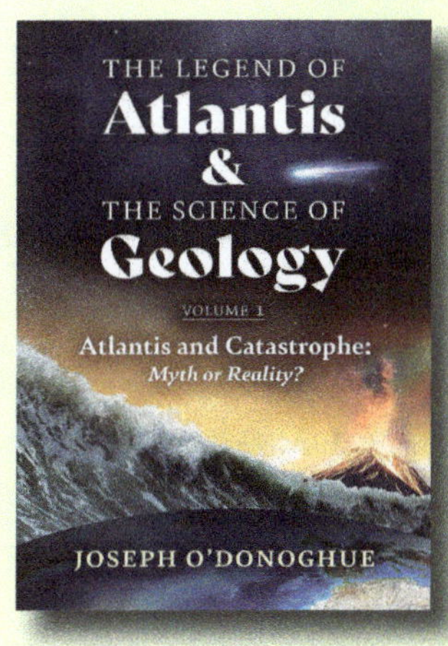

# AUTHOR INTERVIEWS

## What's INSIDE

# TALES AND TALKS

## What's INSIDE

*EDITOR'S CHOICE highlights exceptional books, offering insightful reviews and recommendations to guide readers in discovering their next great read.*

# What's INSIDE

Issue 53 -2025

Scan QR to read online or updated issue.

# From the Editor

Welcome to the 53rd issue of **Reader's House**, a vibrant celebration of literature and the voices that bring unforgettable stories to life. Each issue of our magazine represents a bridge between authors and readers, and we are delighted to present an issue that showcases some of the most diverse, creative, and visionary writers of today.

Gracing our cover is the inspiring Barbara Avon, an award-winning multi-genre author with an extraordinary ability to weave stories that simultaneously haunt and delight. Her journey, from the imaginative musings of a young girl in the Niagara Falls Region to becoming a celebrated author of works like *Revived* and *Sultry Is the Night,* is a testament to passion, perseverance, and a deep belief in the transformative magic of storytelling. In her exclusive interview, Barbara takes us behind the scenes of her creative process, her exploration of themes like love and horror, and the legacy she hopes to leave behind as an author. She invites us into her world, where love and darkness coexist, and where every story is a reflection of the human experience.

This issue is also a tribute to an astounding lineup of literary talent. We are thrilled to feature interviews with over 20 exceptional authors, each with their own unique voice and storytelling mastery. From the evocative imagination of David Gordon to the historical brilliance of Linnea Tanner, and from the cutting-edge narratives of Joseph Schwartz to the heartfelt tales of Ruth Fein, these authors represent the diverse ways in which words can move us, challenge us, and inspire us.

We'd like to highlight the incredible work of all the authors featured in this issue:

David Gordon, Joseph Schwartz, Linnea Tanner, A.D. Vancise, Catalina Dubois, Alexandru Czimbor, Colin Van Dongen, Mia Van Dongen, Budd Titlow, C.R. Fabis, Elaine Patterson, Dr. Ketan Kulkarni, Jobert E. Abueva, Peter Ralston, Gwen McPhail, Deanna Bussadori, Mark Gorkin, Ruth Fein, Shaun Goldsmith, and Sherry Argov.

Their stories and interviews offer a profound insight into the creative process and show us the boundless potential of literature. As we dive into their worlds, we discover tales that range from romance to science fiction, from historical drama to psychological intrigue. Some explore the most intimate facets of humanity, while others take us on grand adventures beyond the stars. With such a wide variety of voices and stories, this issue captures the energy and diversity that define today's literary landscape.

Issue 53 is more than a celebration of writing—it is a testament to the community that literature builds. As you turn these pages, we hope you'll feel inspired by the journeys of the authors we feature, connected to the stories they share, and reminded that the written word has an unparalleled power to transform our lives.

Thank you for supporting these incredible storytellers and for being part of our literary family.

Happy reading!

PUBLISHER: READER'S HOUSE MAGAZINE, A Subsidiary of NewYox Media Group. 200 Suite 134-146 Curtain Road, EC2A 3AR London, United Kingdom t: +44 79 3847 8420
editor@readershouse.co.uk II http://readershouse.co.uk II http://newyox.media
EDITORIAL: Anna Harlowe Editor-in-Chief, Dan Peters, Managing Editor, Ben Alan, Art Editor, Z. Robers , Content Editor.
CONTRIBUTORS Claudine D. Reyes, Mickey Mikkelson, Andrea Piacquadio, Adrian T. Cheng, Donna Schim, Jon Allo, Tim Halloran, Oleg Magni, Amir SeilSepour, Bill Youngblood, Jetty Stutzman, Jimmy Choo, Peter Filinovich.

# Exploring Grief, Resilience, And The Art Of Storytelling

A.D. Vancise discusses her inspirations, writing process, and the emotional depth of her novels, highlighting themes of trauma and resilience.

# A.D. VANCISE

## EXPLORES DARK REALITIES AND HUMAN RESILIENCE

Editor's Desk I London

"When I write, I don't just see the scene—I feel it, like a movie unfolding in my mind."

A.D. Vancise captivates readers with her extraordinary storytelling prowess, seamlessly weaving together elements of mystery, trauma, and resilience. Hailing from a quaint Canadian town, she draws upon the stark beauty of her upbringing to infuse her narratives with authenticity and depth. Vancise's debut novel, *Cry of an Osprey*, not only achieved Amazon bestseller status but also garnered the prestigious Beverly Hills Book Award, showcasing her ability to resonate with audiences on a profound level. Her subsequent work, *Hidden in the Shadows*, further cemented her reputation, earning accolades such as the Gold Award from Literary Titan and rave reviews from critics.

What sets Vancise apart is her unique blend of gripping plotlines and emotional exploration. Through the lens of her compelling characters, she navigates the complexities of human experience, compelling readers to confront uncomfortable truths while remaining thoroughly engaged. As she prepares to unveil sequels to her acclaimed works, anticipation builds for the next chapters in Evie Day's gripping journey and the chilling tales surrounding Memoirs from a Killer.

In this exclusive interview, we delve into Vancise's creative process, the inspirations behind her narratives, and the personal experiences that shape her writing. Join us as we explore the mind of a truly talented author whose works not only entertain but also enlighten, offering a glimpse into the shadows of the human psyche.

**What initially inspired you to write Hidden in the Shadows, and how did the idea for the mysterious photo come about?**

When I was nine, I was rummaging through my grandfather's shoebox of family photos when I came across an image of a woman standing next to a tiny box. It intrigued me—guess I had a thing for mysteries even back then. I asked my papa (that's what I called him) about it, and he promptly stormed out of the room like I'd just asked him to explain the meaning of life. Years later, after he passed, I found the photo again and realized the tiny box was actually a coffin. Turns out, this was his first case as a police officer. My curiosity led me down a research rabbit hole—one that somehow landed me in the dark world of child trafficking. The deeper I dug, the more I couldn't look away. And just like that, Hidden in the Shadows was born.

**Cry of an Osprey is deeply personal and rooted in grief. How did writing it help you navigate your own loss?**

Great question. Writing Cry of an Osprey was cathartic in ways I didn't expect. Oddly, revisiting the hospital scenes wasn't the hardest part—I'd already lived those moments. What really gutted me was writing about my brother and his first love, knowing they'd never get their second chance. I don't think grief is something you fully navigate; it's more like you learn how to carry it. But writing helped me put some of that weight onto paper, and for that, I'm grateful.

A.D. Vancise's exceptional talent and poignant storytelling engage readers, inviting them into profound narratives filled with emotion and complexity.

**Your books explore heavy themes such as trauma, love, and resilience. How do you balance these intense subjects while keeping readers engaged?**

I think weaving in humor—when appropriate—helps, along with using dual POVs. In Cry of an Osprey, Amelia's heavy moments are balanced with Ben's more lighthearted or reflective ones. In Hidden in the Shadows, Evie's mystery-driven journey provides relief from the darker, more disturbing scenes surrounding Charlie Baker. It's all about pacing, ending a chapter on an unfinished thought or scene, and knowing when the reader needs a breath. I want them to feel deeply, but I also want them to keep turning the pages.

**Evie Day is a compelling protagonist in Hidden in the Shadows. What aspects of her character do you relate to the most?**

Her naivety, for sure. Her tenacity for truth. And her unwavering belief that people—especially the ones we love—are inherently good. That last one can be a strength or a flaw, depending on the situation.

**You are currently working on sequels to Hidden in the Shadows and Memoirs from a Killer. Can you give us any hints about what readers can expect?**

Absolutely. The next book in the series, Behind the Shadows, follows Evie as she fights against an untouchable trafficking network after her nine-year-old son, L.J., is kidnapped. But L.J. isn't just a victim—he's outsmarting them from the inside. Just as Evie gets close to rescuing him, betrayal strikes, and she's killed... or so it seems. A shadowy figure from her past has been watching, and he's not ready to let her die just yet.

Memoirs from a Killer is a prequel to Hidden in the Shadows, narrated by Roman, a character from the first book. And here's where things get wild—I'm working with a medium from California who is channeling a man with a story to tell. Sounds crazy, right? But here's a teaser:

"History is written by the victors. But the real story is buried in the dead—etched in skin like aged leather, in bones brittle as a boiled carcass, and in eyes that have witnessed centuries of horror. This is my story, the one they never wanted you to hear."

**As a visual artist as well as a writer, do you find that your artistic background influences your storytelling or the way you visualise scenes?**

One hundred percent! When I write, I don't just see the scene—I feel it, like a movie unfolding in my mind. I think that's the artist in me, helping to shape the atmosphere with details that bring the world to life. My writing has been described as cinematic and atmospheric, and I definitely credit my artistic background for that.

**Having grown up in a small town, how has your upbringing and connection to place shaped your writing?**

Growing up on a farm in the middle of nowhere gave me plenty of time to read (and no Wi-Fi, so books were my escape). But more than that, being surrounded by nature, animals, and quiet moments allowed my imagination to run wild. I'd take myself on mysterious journeys through the wheat fields, forests, and into the barn, inventing stories as I went. That ability to lose myself in another world? It stuck with me.

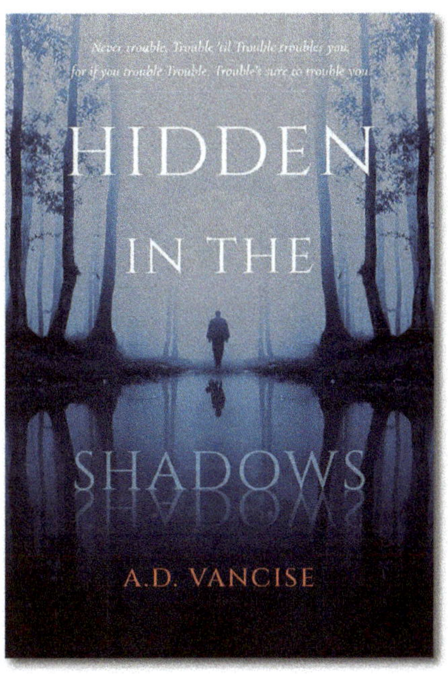


Michael Goddart's *The Contentment Dividend* offers 49 meditations guiding readers toward spiritual self-discovery, inner peace, and divine connection. Rooted in teachings from realised Masters and Saints, it helps quiet the mind, access higher wisdom, and cultivate contentment. The book encourages reflection, receptivity to grace, and a deeper understanding of existence.

**What advice would you give to aspiring authors who are struggling to share their personal stories or take the first step in writing their book?**

Read—a lot. And not just in your favorite genre. Read everything to understand different writing styles, pacing, and storytelling techniques. Pay attention to reader reviews; they're gold when it comes to learning what resonates and what doesn't. Take writing courses, and most importantly, be open to criticism. It's not the enemy—it's the catalyst for better writing. And forget about the pressure of publishing. Write because you love to write. Your story matters.

# Exploring The Intersection Of Technology, Philosophy, And Human Nature Through Engaging Storytelling

Alexandru Czimbor discusses his literary journey, the influences behind his award-winning novels, and the intricate themes of technology and human consciousness.

# ALEXANDRU CZIMBOR

## UNVEILS THE DEPTHS OF HUMANITY IN HIS GROUNDBREAKING NOVELS

Editor's Desk I London

"Having experienced life under this regime, I aspire to expose in my writing the hypocrisy of both far-left and far-right governments.

Alexandru Czimbor stands as a luminous beacon in contemporary literature, merging the realms of technology and storytelling with an unparalleled finesse. An accomplished author and seasoned executive, his dual expertise enriches his narratives, inviting readers to explore the intricate interplay between human consciousness and artificial intelligence. Czimbor's career, spanning over two decades within the Information Technology sector, finds harmonious expression in his novels, most notably in the award-winning *The Soul Machines and Sentience Hazard*.

His literary journey is marked by a profound exploration of philosophical and societal themes, reminiscent of his upbringing in Transylvania during the repressive regime of Nicolae Ceaușescu. This unique perspective imbues his works with a critical lens on the human condition, often reflecting on the historical and contemporary struggles between ideology and individuality. Czimbor's ability to weave complex characters within richly imagined worlds has garnered him significant acclaim, a testament to his skill in crafting narratives that resonate deeply with readers.

*The Soul Machines*, an evocative blend of historical fiction and mystery, has captivated audiences and critics alike, earning prestigious awards such as the Literary Titan Gold Award and the Pinnacle Book Achievement Award. Its successor, *Sentience Hazard*, further solidifies Czimbor's reputation, delving into the ethical complexities of artificial intelligence—an area he approaches with both intellectual curiosity and personal insight.

This interview delves into Alexandru Czimbor's motivations, experiences, and the nuanced themes that permeate his work, offering a rare glimpse into the mind of a writer who deftly navigates the intersections of technology, philosophy, and human emotion. As we celebrate his achievements and visionary storytelling, it becomes clear that Czimbor is not only a voice of our times but also a prescient guide to the future interconnections of humanity and its creations.

### How did your upbringing in Transylvania during Nicolae Ceaușescu's regime influence the themes in your novels?

Ceaușescu came to power in 1965, leading a totalitarian government that combined the communist ideals with a cult of personality, strong nationalism, and political repression. Growing up in that environment, I learned to keep my thoughts, words, and actions separate. When I was old enough to understand more, my mother opened my eyes to the lies of the system. I became suspicious of the constant propaganda and of the pretense of teachers and others. I forced myself to distinguish between reality and hollow words. Having experienced life under this regime, I aspire to expose in my writing the hypocrisy of both far-left and far-right governments. I want to warn readers, especially those who take freedom for granted, mesmerized by the promises of a utopian society, that the dark side of human nature can push us back into the abyss of oppression at any time.

**"*The Soul Machines*" intertwines historical truth with imagination. What inspired you to set this story in 19th-century Transylvania?**

The end of the 19th century and at the dawn of the 20th century were shaped by extreme ideology. The idealization of the oppressed led to communism and nationalism paved the way for fascism. I noticed the unfortunate similarities between the societal turmoil of that time and the disturbance of our age. Once again, we witness the exacerbation of extreme thinking in politics, a deep division in society, and the acute loss of common sense.

Transylvania was an ideal setting for this novel, both because I was born there and I know it well, and because it represents a melting pot of ethnic groups, including Romanians, Hungarians, Saxon Germans, and Gypsies. I wanted to illustrate how people of different origins, races, and social classes can coexist, despite all the life challenges. The Soul Machines is a call for a return to the political center and to the core values that unite us.

> Alexandru Czimbor's masterful storytelling and profound insights into human nature elevate him as a truly remarkable voice in contemporary literature.

**In "*Sentience Hazard,*" you explore the boundaries between human and machine. How does your background in computer science inform this narrative?**

I became passionate about Artificial Intelligence in the '80s. My mother used to work for the Computing Center of the Romanian Post. One day, while visiting her, I was introduced to one of the first chatbots created at MIT, which had made its way into the computers available there. The idea of a virtual "person" with whom I could converse immediately captured my imagination. The desire to learn more about AI was one of the main reasons I pursued computer science. Since then, I have read extensively on the topic and gained a deeper appreciation and respect for the complexity of the human mind.

We are now experiencing an AI resurgence, due to the unexpected success of generative AI. Just like, as a child, I was lured by the illusion of a conscious being chatting with me, today we routinely anthropomorphize tools like ChatGPT. We speak of computer programs displaying "general intelligence," "creativity," "will," or "consciousness." With Sentience Hazard, I wanted to show both how far we are from true, human-like intelligence, and how machine intelligence, if unchecked or exploited by malicious actors, can have devastating consequences.

**Your novels blend genres like fantasy, mystery, and historical fiction. How do you approach combining these elements in your storytelling?**

I like to make my fiction as plausible as possible.

In The Soul Machines, I intertwined elements of mystery and a touch of fantasy with the realities of 19th-century Transylvania. My goal wasn't to create a fantasy novel but to craft a believable story with exceptional characters driven by love, hatred, loyalty, and passion. The "machines" that amplify human emotions merely symbolize the corruption of our souls, while I built the story around the people influenced by them.

Sentience Hazard is more clearly defined as a specific genre, but in it, too, I aimed to present the development of AI and the global tension as they impact people's lives.

**Themes such as the rise of extreme politics and the conflict between religion and naturalism are present in your work. What draws you to these subjects?**

Our propensity to create stories for phenomena that we can't understand has always fascinated me. Religions are full of powerful stories, some of which should be taken literally and others figuratively. Over the last couple of centuries, we've made incredible scientific progress. We now find ourselves trapped in this perpetual dance between reason and faith. As humans, we are inexorably drawn to a belief system, whether based on the supernatural or on intellect. Once committed to it, we lose objectivity. I challenge my readers to question their beliefs, especially the ones they are most sure of, and to try to understand the perspectives of those they disagree with.

**How has your experience in academia and the software industry influenced your writing process and the subjects you choose to explore?**

Throughout my career, I've worked in many different environments—teaching, programming, entrepreneurship, management. I've launched software products and led teams providing software development services for large U.S. companies. This broad experience has allowed me to meet people from all kinds of backgrounds, giving me a strong understanding of how people think, feel, and act. This helps shape my writing.

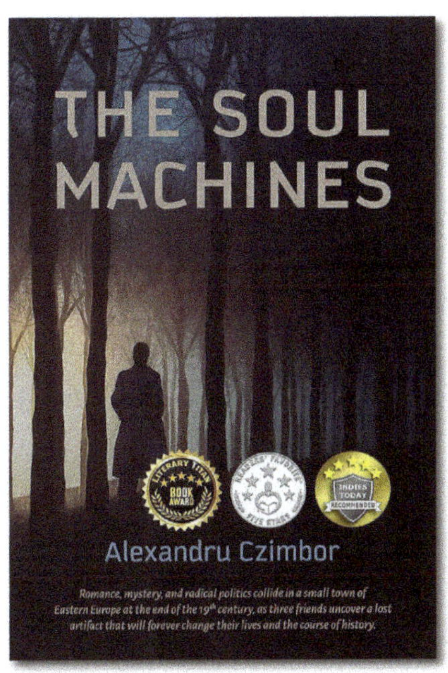


> *The Soul Machines* by Alexandru Czimbor is a compelling tale set in 19th-century Transylvania, exploring friendship amid societal strife. With themes of political extremism and forbidden love, the narrative weaves romance and mystery seamlessly. Czimbor's evocative prose captures the era's turmoil, making this a thought-provoking read. Highly recommended.

**Your books have received several awards. How have these accolades impacted your career and approach to writing?**

When I started writing, I hardly had any readers. I submitted my work to various writing competitions mainly to attract more. I am both surprised and overjoyed that my novels have placed highly in so many prestigious competitions. Literary awards certainly make me set a higher standard for myself.

**What advice would you give to aspiring authors who wish to blend complex themes into their narratives?**

Authors who want to tackle complex topics should read across a variety of genres to widen their horizons. They need to understand the bigger picture, yet be able to focus on relevant details. They need to hone their inquisitive skills and choose their subjects carefully. Then, they should fully commit to the creative process.

# Championing Conservation Through Words and Images

Award-winning author Budd Titlow discusses his latest book Coming Full Circle, his passion for conservation, the power of photography in storytelling, and the urgent need for environmental action through historical and factual narratives.

# BUDD TITLOW

## INSPIRES READERS WITH A POWERFUL BLEND OF CONSERVATION, HISTORY, AND STORYTELLING IN HIS LATEST WORKS

"Both Mariah and I are lifelong conservationists, so combining our knowledge for this book just made sense."

Editor's Desk I London

Budd Titlow is more than just an author—he is a passionate storyteller, an esteemed wildlife ecologist, and a devoted conservationist who has spent decades bringing the wonders of the natural world to life through his words and photographs. With an unwavering commitment to environmental awareness, his work serves as both a call to action and a celebration of the beauty that surrounds us.

His latest book, *Coming Full Circle: How Americans Finally Got Things Right!*, is a masterful blend of historical fiction and environmental insight, offering readers a thought-provoking journey through time. With a narrative that interweaves real-world challenges and triumphs, Titlow crafts a compelling vision of hope—one that urges us to reflect on our past to shape a better future. This book joins his impressive repertoire, which includes *Protecting the Planet: Environmental Champions from Conservation to Climate Change*, *Bird Brains*, and *Seashells*, each showcasing his ability to illuminate the intricate relationships between humans and nature.

With over 500 published photo-essays, 5,000 photographs, and eight books to his name, Titlow's work is a testament to the power of storytelling in the fight for conservation. His expertise and passion have earned him critical acclaim, with *Coming Full Circle* hailed as an "adventurous, passionate historical novel" by *Kirkus Reviews* and a "highly recommended read" by the *US Review of Books.*

In this interview, Budd Titlow shares insights into his creative process, the inspirations behind his works, and the urgent need for environmental stewardship. His journey as an author and conservationist is nothing short of remarkable, and his message is one that resonates now more than ever.

**In *"PROTECTING THE PLANET,"* you highlight environmental champions. How did collaborating with your daughter, Mariah Tinger, influence the narrative?**

Both Mariah and I are life-long conservationists and environmental activists, so combining our knowledge for this book just made sense.

***"BIRD BRAINS"* delves into the avian mind. What inspired you to explore the "thinking" abilities of birds in this book?**

Using both photos and words, "Bird Brains"depicts unusual — and sometimes just plain crazy — actions I have seen 100 wild birds take during my 40-year career working in the field.

> Budd Titlow masterfully blends science, history, and storytelling, inspiring readers to embrace environmental stewardship and appreciate the beauty of our natural world.

**Your book *"SEASHELLS—Jewels from the Ocean"* showcases mollusks across the world. How did your background as a wildlife biologist inform your approach to this subject?**

In reality, I had minimal personal experience with mollusks. An editor with Voyageur Press — who knew that I specialized in both writing and photography — called me "out of the blue" — and asked me to produce this book. It has actually sold pretty well!

**In *"ROCKY MOUNTAIN NATIONAL PARK—Beyond Trail Ridge,"* you present unique perspectives. What challenges did you face capturing the park's essence beyond popular trails?**

During my 13 years living in Colorado, I spent a lot of time working with the book's photographers to learn about "RMNP's" backcountry.

**Your *"Life Shots"* gallery offers a preview of your work. How does this collection complement the themes explored in your books?**

As both a freelance writer and photographer, I have always used my photographic experiences to inspire my writing.

**As an award-winning nature photographer, how do your photographic experiences influence your writing, particularly in your recent publications?**

My two latest books — both addressing our daunting environmental threats of climate change and biodiversity loss — are primarily narrative only (one non-fiction and one fiction), but they are both based on my love of and appreciation for the natural world gained through my photography.

**Your presentations cover topics from bird behaviour to environmental conservation. How do these engagements enrich your writing process?**

Aside from my family, my greatest pleasure in life is sharing my experiences with the natural world through my Power Point presentations!

**What key advice would you offer aspiring authors aiming to write about natural history and environmental conservation?**

Write about what you know and love and DON'T EVER GIVE UP!

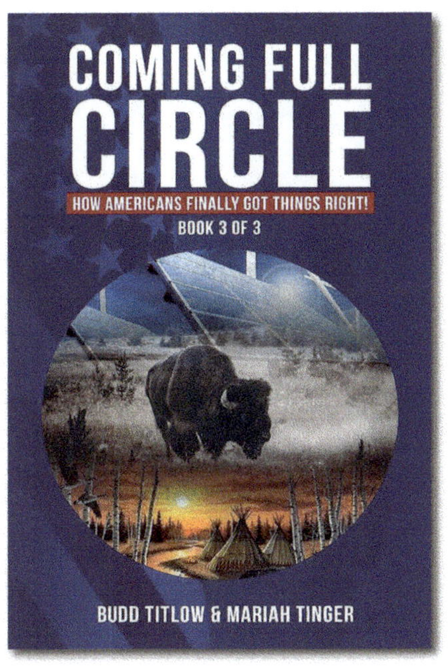


> *Coming Full Circle: How Americans Finally Got Things Right!* – (Volumes 1- 3) by Budd Titlow and Mariah Tinger is a compelling historical novel exploring humanity's relationship with nature. Through diverse characters and rich storytelling, it highlights past lessons, environmental urgency, and hope for change, offering an inspiring call to action.

The most important thing is to avoid becoming so mired in historical details that your story begins to read like a textbook."

## Fiction That Challenges, Inspires, and Resonates Across Generations

Catalina DuBois masterfully blends historical fiction with social insight, exploring interracial love, forgotten histories, and the resilience of the human spirit through meticulous research and fearless storytelling.

# CATALINA DUBOIS

## EXPLORES LOVE, HISTORY, AND THE POWER OF STORYTELLING

Editor's Desk I London

Catalina DuBois, a luminary in contemporary literature, has captivated readers with her profoundly resonant narratives that explore the intricate tapestry of American history through the lens of personal experience and cultural identity. Since the publication of her debut novel in 2009, DuBois has distinguished herself not only as a talented storyteller but also as a passionate advocate for the acknowledgement of the multifaceted aspects of history that shape our understanding of the present. Her works, adorned with numerous accolades, delve into the dynamics of interracial relationships while illuminating the struggles of those who have navigated the often turbulent waters of societal change.

In this issue of Reader's House magazine, we are thrilled to present an insightful interview with DuBois, wherein she shares the inspirations behind her writing and offers a glimpse into her creative process. Her insightful reflections challenge the conventional narratives that often obscure the rich diversity of experiences within American history. With eloquence and conviction, she invites us to reconsider preconceived notions and to embrace a more inclusive understanding of our collective past.

DuBois's commitment to authenticity is evident in her meticulous research, drawing from both historical resources and the invaluable wisdom of elders, whose stories enrich her narratives with depth and truth. As her readers have found, her tales are far more than mere historical fiction; they are lessons embedded in rich storytelling, reflective of her profound respect for the art of African storytelling that has influenced her approach.

Join us in celebrating the remarkable journey of Catalina DuBois, whose voice continues to resonate across borders, encouraging readers worldwide to engage with history in a meaningful way. With each book, she not only entertains but challenges us all to reflect more deeply on the legacies that shape our lives today.

**What inspired you to explore historical themes through fiction, particularly focusing on interracial relationships and the challenges faced in different time periods?**

After meeting the love of my life I began to wonder if things may have gone differently for us had we been born just fifty years sooner. Would the world have graciously bestowed blessings upon our love, or would fifty years, a mere blink in time have made us tragically star crossed? If we would have been cursed over so small a change, how would a hundred years affect us or a thousand?

> DuBois crafts immersive, thought-provoking narratives that challenge historical misconceptions while delivering deeply emotional and compelling storytelling.

**How do you balance historical accuracy with creative storytelling when writing your novels?**

The most important thing is to avoid becoming so mired in historical details that your story begins to read like a textbook.

**What kind of research process do you undertake to ensure your depiction of historical events and cultures is authentic?**

Libraries are an abundant resource. I also enjoy traveling to museums and historical sites. My absolute favorite method of research is to interview my elders for firsthand accounts of historical events. There are so many uncomfortable truths and politically incorrect details that never make it into history books. Human beings are the best source of knowledge because older folks don't care about your feelings. They speak the truth and I love them for it.

**Your books have received international recognition—how do you think perspectives on American history differ between audiences in the U.S. and abroad?**

One thing I prefer about an international audience is the open-mindedness and the absence of racism. They don't carve up American history into subcategories based on race to exclude entire ethnic groups in a phony revisionist fairytale that we force-feed to school children. These lies are spread by Americans alone and they sicken me. I love an international audience because they see us all as Americans. There is no black history nor women's history on a world stage. It's all American history.

**What challenges have you faced in addressing sensitive historical topics, and how do you navigate criticism while staying true to your vision?**

Long ago I accepted the fact that I can't please everyone. Anytime you tell the truth it angers immature people. They were raised inside a shell of ignorance and fluffy delusions. The truth is the breaking of that shell. It is a painful but necessary transition on the journey to understanding our past and shaping a brighter future for all.

**Can you share more about your experience with African storytelling and how it influenced your writing style and themes?**

African tales are rarely just to entertain you. There is usually a lesson to be learned. To remain true to this tradition my books have societal lessons within them. I have the greatest respect for African storytelling. It's one of the precious few customs that made it across the Atlantic. I gaze in the mirror knowing that I have lost my name, my language, my religion, and even my skin color as I have been mixed into the beautiful melting pot that is America. But the one thing I will always have is those stories that filled my heart as a child. Those stories made me a blend of two worlds and I will always try to honor them.

Sara, a Nubian princess, is destined to become Pharaoh's fifth wife, but her heart belongs to Matthaios, a foreign slave. As duty clashes with love, she must choose between power and passion. Catalina DuBois' novel explores romance, sacrifice, and defiance in a vividly depicted ancient Egyptian setting.

> "Each dessert I created had its own story."

# Blending Fact, Fiction, and Imagination

Award-winning author C.R. Fabis discusses his dynamic journey from dessert chef to novelist, shares insights into his creative process, and explores the themes and characters that define his extraordinary work.

# C.R. FABIS

## TAKES READERS ON AN UNFORGETTABLE JOURNEY THROUGH HISTORY, MORALITY, AND CREATIVITY

Editor's Desk I London

C.R. Fabis emerges as a singular talent in the literary world, defying convention and showcasing a remarkable capacity to craft stories that captivate, challenge, and inspire. Known to many as an accomplished dessert chef whose creations once delighted palates across the United States, Fabis transitioned into the world of storytelling with the same ingenuity and passion he brought to the culinary arts. His debut novel, *Rome Never Fell*, a bold fusion of historical fiction and science fiction, marked his arrival as a novelist of extraordinary vision and depth. With his follow-up, *The Angel and the Amazing Life of Maggie Love*, he demonstrated yet again his ability to weave compelling narratives that grapple with complex themes, leaving readers enthralled and contemplative in equal measure.

An undeniable polymath, C.R. Fabis also delights audiences as a cartoonist on Instagram, where his visual work brims with humour and creativity. Yet it is in his prose that he finds his full range of expression, crafting intricate characters and plots with spontaneity and authenticity. Whether imagining time travel to ancient Rome or exploring the moral ambiguities of revenge through the enigmatic Maggie Love, Fabis's work speaks to a unique mind unafraid to traverse the boundaries of genre and artistry.

It is a rare privilege to spotlight a voice as dynamic as C.R. Fabis in this issue of *Reader's House*. In this exclusive interview, we delve into his transition from the culinary world to literature, the inspirations behind his unforgettable characters, and his advice for aspiring authors. Join us as we uncover the creative journey of an author who dares to blend the extraordinary with the everyday, proving that storytelling, like dessert, is truly an art.

### What inspired you to transition from a successful career as a dessert chef to writing novels?

I worked for a big dessert company for 25 years. When the company sold, it was time for retirement. I worked out a good deal with this company, so I am financially sound. I have always had stories in my head. You might say that each dessert I created had its own story. When my children were young, I made up bedtime stories for them. A few years later I wrote those down as a novel. Now, I knew I could do it, so the transition to writing was quite easy.

### How do your experiences in the culinary world influence the themes or characters in your books?

Most of the chefs I have known over the years have strange and quirky personalities. Some were warm and helpful, and some could be mean and self-centered. I have been able to use pieces of these personalities in many of the characters I have created in my books. I have found that the dark personalities can be the most interesting, and the most fun to write about.

C.R. Fabis masterfully combines vivid imagination, nuanced characters, and genre-defying narratives, proving himself to be a storytelling virtuoso.

### In "Rome Never Fell," you blend historical fiction with science fiction. What challenges did you face in merging these genres?

Since time travel is the science fiction, and going back to a historic time was the historical fiction, the merging of the genres worked well. The challenge I had was the research needed. I wanted my interpretation of Julius Caesar, Mark Antony, Cleopatra, and others to be as accurate and real as possible. I needed to know exactly how these events of their time happened. So, my study of this amazing time in human history made the story real and even plausible.

### "The Angel and the Amazing Life of Maggie Love" delves into complex moral questions. What motivated you to explore such themes?

It is extremely hard to justify murder, even in literature. But it is much easier for the reader to accept it if there is a revenge factor involved. You see this in the cinema all the time. That is where my motivation came from. Maggie was dealt a bad deck as a child. She is beautiful, brilliant, and well-motivated to get revenge on those who wronged her. An Angel, along with the reader, has to decide if revenge is enough justification to save her soul.

### As a cartoonist with a substantial following on Instagram, how does your visual art background inform your storytelling?

First of all, the cartoons are stories. Before I can make a cartoon, there has to be a story, and it has to be visual in my head. I cannot emphasize this enough. Whether it is a novel, a cartoon or any other creative endeavor, the story has to be visual in the author's head. This makes it real to me and I always hope it makes it real to my readers. My Instagram following likes my cartoons because they make them laugh. This makes me happy, but the best part of making them is that they make me laugh.

### Could you share insights into your writing process, particularly how you develop your characters and plotlines?

When I sit down to start a novel, I have to have a basic idea of who the characters are and where the story is going. It is especially important that I have a slightly vague idea of how it is going to end. To me, the writing process is very spontaneous. I do not make any outlines of what the book is supposed to be. Plot twists and surprises come to me while I am writing. Sometimes when I go to sleep, I might get an idea. I might be out for a walk and something happens. In other words, I become completely ingulfed in the story I'm writing. It is a 24/7 process, where a little bit of magic can happen at any time.

### What advice would you offer to aspiring authors looking to blend elements from different creative fields into their writing?

If an inspiring author has experience in other creative fields, odds are they have already created something different. Most of my successful desserts were quite different for their time. Do not try to be like Hemingway, or Rowling. Do not read a mystery novel and then try to write like that author. Try to capture whatever creative spark you had in your field. Use this spark in your writing to create something different. Use it in your plot development, and your characters. Make your story as real as possible in your own head. That way it will be very real to your readers.

### In your book, "The Angel and the Amazing Life of Maggie Love", what do you think makes Maggie Love such a compelling character?

In chapter 3, Maggie's parents were forced into murder suicide by some evil people. This gives her a kind of vague justification for all the murders she is going to commit. She develops a sense of humor. She uses her intelligence and beauty to help her get things done. She is very self-determined. She can change her appearance constantly using wigs, different colored contact lenses, different voices, and fashion and thus, she has 12 aliases. Most people would agree that a woman who has committed 20 murders would be a compelling character.

C. R. Fabis weaves a captivating tale in *The Angel and the Amazing Life of Maggie Love.* A unique blend of mystery and the metaphysical, the novel explores morality and redemption through Maggie, a complex anti-heroine. Thought-provoking and original, it compels readers to question good versus evil. Highly recommended for introspective thrill-seekers!

# A Beloved Father-Daughter Duo Inspiring Young Minds

Colin and Mia van Dongen discuss their creative journey, sharing insights on storytelling, collaboration, and the joys of their beloved Winston the Titan Terrier series.

# COLIN & MIA VAN DONGEN

## UNVEIL THE MAGIC OF STORYTELLING

Editor's Desk I London

"Mia: The idea of it sounded really exciting! Since the book came out, I feel more confident..."

Colin van Dongen stands as a testament to the power of creativity and connection, weaving together the realms of storytelling and innovation in a manner that captivates audiences of all ages. An award-winning storyteller and visionary, he has navigated a rich tapestry of careers, from oceanography to the vibrant world of animation and advertising. However, it is his unique partnership with his daughter, Mia, that has truly redefined his creative journey. Together, they have embarked on an extraordinary adventure, co-authoring the beloved Winston the Titan Terrier series. What began as a playful collaboration has blossomed into a profound exploration of storytelling, igniting imaginations and enriching their lives in ways that extend far beyond the written word.

Mia van Dongen, an award-winning young storyteller in her own right, brings a spark of joy and authenticity to their collaborative works. Despite her tender age, she demonstrates an impressive command of narrative and creativity, inviting young readers into a world filled with adventure and heart. The stories of Winston, a brave Boston Terrier guided by a celestial guardian, resonate deeply with children, encouraging them to explore their own imaginations while embracing valuable lessons about friendship and resilience.

As they prepare to release the next installment in their series, Winston the Titan Terrier: Adventures in Ancient Egypt, Colin and Mia reflect on their creative synergy and the profound impact that unplugging from digital distractions has had on their lives. Their insights, shared in this exclusive interview, reveal not only the joys and challenges of co-authoring as a parent and child but also their commitment to fostering a love of reading and learning in young minds. Readers will find inspiration in their journey, as well as practical wisdom for nurturing creativity in their own families.

Join us as we delve into the hearts and minds of Colin and Mia van Dongen, celebrating their remarkable achievements and the magic they continue to create together through the power of storytelling.

### What inspired you both to start writing the Winston The Titan Terrier series together, and how did the idea first come about?

Mia (7): When my mom went out shopping and I was watching TV at home, my dad said to me, "Let's write a book together?" The idea of it sounded really exciting! Since the book came out, I feel more confident and have made some great friends. Sometimes, kids I don't even know come up to me and tell me how much they love it, and want to talk about their favourite character in the book which has been really cool! I have had so much fun creating these books with my dad.

Colin : I saw my parents collaborating on a children's book together when I was young which was a factor. However, one of the main influences that initiated this project was a quote I saw from an author, Glennon Doyle, who inspired us to take a more balanced approach to technology in our home.

"I find myself worrying most that when we hand our children phones, we steal their boredom from them. As a result, we are raising a generation of writers who will never start writing, artists who will never start doodling, chefs who will never make a mess in the kitchen, athletes who will never kick a ball against a wall, musicians who will never pick up their aunt's guitar and start strumming."

**Mia, as such a young author when you started this project as a 5 year old, what has been the most exciting part of creating stories with your dad?**

I loved seeing all the pictures being made by my dad, and seeing the story unfold from the book's first storyboards. One of the most exciting moments was finding out we won a Gold Literary Titan Award in America and being the first person at my school to get the "Agent of Change" badge from my principal for students who are making a positive impact in our world!

Colin van Dongen's innovative storytelling and inspiring partnership with Mia showcase his dedication to nurturing creativity and imagination in children's literature.

**Colin, how has collaborating with Mia on these books influenced your perspective on storytelling and creativity?**

Collaborating with Mia on these books has been both humbling and inspiring. Watching her imagination flourish from ages five to seven as she brought these worlds to life has been a privilege. Over time, I realised that her ideas were often far better than mine, and I had to step outside my own box to fully embrace the imaginative world she was creating and join in on the ride.

Completing Winston the Titan Terrier: The Cosmic Bone broke many barriers for us, proving that anything is possible as authors. We're thrilled to announce that the next installment in the series, Winston the Titan Terrier: Adventures in Ancient Egypt, will be released in June 2025. This will push the envelope even further in terms of the plot and the illustrations.

Mia and many friends have encouraged me to publish a memoir called "9 Lives", which will detail my adventures and many near death experiences as an extreme sports enthusiast and professional surf videographer. While navigating the unpredictable rollercoaster ride as an insulin-dependent diabetic.

**The Winston series blends adventure, problem solving, and fun characters. What message do you hope young readers take away from these stories?**

The series echoes the message of never giving up and the power of friendship. Through Winston's journeys, young readers learn that even the biggest challenges can be overcome with determination, looking for solutions, and the support of friends and family.

**Beyond writing, you've also developed WinstonBooks.com. How does this platform enhance the reading experience for children and families?**

One of the greatest rewards of working with Mia was quality time away from screens. To promote this, we created WinstonBooks.com, offering educational toys, activities, and books, including our future books and those by other authors.

Mia, do you have a favourite moment or character in The Cosmic Bone, and what makes it special to you? My favourite character is Winston because he is based on my real dog! He is really adorable, super cute and I just really love him so much! I have had him as my dog since I was a baby. His personality closely matches the character as he has a love for sports, adventure, and all kinds of food and snacks!

My favourite scene in the Cosmic Bone is when Winston uses his Bubblegum Cannon to stop Smokestrike in the tunnels under the Bone Shop. I love rainbows, so I imagined colourful bubblegum balls that could be fired and trap the naughty Ninja Cat!

Colin, your background spans multiple creative industries. How have these experiences shaped your approach to children's literature? One of the scenes features a monstrous wave that was deployed by Smokestrike that was about to crash on Winston. This was drawn from my own experiences as a water cameraman, where I've often found myself in many similar positions to capture wave riders in dangerous conditions. The intensity and the danger of those moments influenced the tension of that particular scene.

In terms of production, I was lucky enough to apply over 25 years of design and animation experience to this project, using both classic 3D modelling and new emerging technology to build dynamic compositions that brought Mia's story to life.

*Winston The Titan Terrier - The Cosmic Bone* is a delightful adventure that captivates both children and adults alike. With vibrant illustrations and a thrilling narrative, Winston's quest to reclaim his cosmic bone is filled with clever inventions and unexpected allies. A heartwarming tale of camaraderie and creativity!

**What advice would you give to other authors, especially those looking to collaborate with young writers on storytelling projects?**

Embrace flexibility and creativity. Start with quick, rough storyboarding to capture ideas quickly without interrupting the flow of imagination of a younger storyteller. It's important to establish clear boundaries to ensure a logical progression from beginning to end. Take the time to explore different possibilities for plot themes and character development, and don't rush the process. Seek out negative feedback and suggestions from trusted sources, those comments are gold.

Role-playing sparked a wave of creativity in our 2nd book when we transformed Mia's grumpy toy octopus into a future villain, known as SadFace. This toy character brought endless laughs and inspired fresh ideas for our next installment. Winston the Titan Terrier: Adventures in Ancient Egypt, where SadFace uses a time twister device to unleash chaos by teleporting gigantic prehistoric dinosaurs into Queen Cleopatra's timeline, while Winston tries to save Egypt and the universe...

# Mystery, Horror, and Sci-Fi Collide in Gordon's Novels

David Gordon, an award-winning author, masterfully blends history, science fiction, and mystery. In this interview, he discusses time travel, historical accuracy, creative storytelling, and offers valuable advice for aspiring writers.

# DAVID GORDON

## WEAVES HISTORY, MYSTERY, AND SCIENCE FICTION INTO UNFORGETTABLE STORIES

Editor's Desk I London

"Time travel is pivotal to my novels, influencing both plot and character development as heroes and villains reshape reality."

David Gordon is an award-winning writer whose mastery of historical fiction, science fiction, and mystery has captivated readers worldwide. With a background in education as a social studies teacher, principal, and founder of the Grand Canyon College Preparatory Academy, Gordon infuses his novels with both thrilling adventure and historical depth. His passion for blending history with speculative fiction has given rise to unforgettable series such as *Jigsaw, Case File,* and *Moly*—each transporting readers into the past with a twist of the extraordinary.

Gordon's *Jigsaw* series is an exhilarating dive into history's forgotten moments, reimagining the past through the lens of time-traveling teens who uncover secrets that never made it into textbooks. His love for classic science fiction and horror is evident in every carefully crafted narrative, with influences ranging from Bradbury to *Doctor Who* and *Star Trek.* Whether exploring the origins of Batman and Universal Horror in *Jigsaw: History's Forgotten* or delving into noir-inspired mystery horror in *The Mummy's Vengeance*, Gordon's ability to fuse fact with fiction is nothing short of remarkable.

Beyond his novels, Gordon's commitment to historical accuracy and immersive storytelling shines through in his meticulous research, ensuring that readers not only embark on thrilling adventures but also gain insights into real historical events—many of which remain overlooked. His latest work, *The Trail of the Zombies*, sheds light on the harrowing experiences of Native American children in government-run schools, blending supernatural intrigue with historical truth.

In this exclusive interview, David Gordon discusses the inspirations behind his work, the intricate role of time travel in shaping his narratives, and the dedication required to balance creative freedom with historical fidelity. A champion of perseverance, he also shares invaluable advice for aspiring authors eager to make their mark in science fiction and historical fiction.

Reader's House is proud to present this conversation with David Gordon, a writer whose stories do more than entertain—they challenge, educate, and invite us to reconsider the past through the lens of the extraordinary.

**What inspired you to blend science fiction, fantasy, and historical fiction in your Jigsaw series?**

Excellent question. I am a semi-retired educator who started out as a History Teacher. When you combine that background with my passion for science fiction, historical fiction, and mystery horror, the list of story possibilities is endless. I was heavily influenced by stories like Bradbury's The Sound of Thunder, Christies Ten Little Indians, and Michener's The Source as well as the best Star Trek, Doctor Who, Twilight Zone, Outer Limits, and Universal Horror.

**Could you elaborate on the role of time travel in your novels and how it influences the characters' development?**

David Gordon is a literary visionary whose compelling storytelling fuses history, science fiction, and mystery into unforgettable, thought-provoking adventures.

In my Jigsaw series, time travel is pivotal to the plot of the novels, and it also lends insights into the protagonists and antagonists character development because our main heroes and villains make their decisions based on how they want to maintain or alter reality to their own ends.

**How do you balance historical accuracy with creative storytelling in your works?**

For the reader, I have two goals when I am writing. One is to be entertaining by writing an exciting plot and character driven story. The second goal in the time traveling series is to be educational. It is very important that the historical setting and characters are as accurate as possible because I want my readers to learn about actual historical events like how there was an effective Italian Resistance in World War Two or American Women in Space Program in the late 1950's and early 1960's or how the movie The Man Who Laughs influenced the creation of the Joker in the Batman comics or even in my latest mystery-horror book, The Trail of the Zombies where I describe the plight of Native American children in government run schools at the turn of the twentieth century.

**What challenges did you face when writing "The Mummy's Vengeance," and how did you overcome them?**

After writing six time travel centered stories, The Mummy's Vengeance, my first mystery-horror was actually fairly easy to do. It actually took me less than six weeks to write the first draft whereas it takes me a little over two months to write a time travel novella. What I wanted to do there was write a 1920's-30's noir piece that was a tribute to both the Universal Horror Classics and works of Christie and Hammett.

**In "Jigsaw: History's Forgotten," you explore various historical events. Which event did you find most intriguing to write about?**

I liked the historical cause and effect premise of the second History's Forgotten Part Two where our antagonists, having failed to stop the creation of Batman and the Universal Horror franchise in Part One, attempted to change history by, in part eliminating I Love Lucy's cinematographer Karl Freund on the Eastern Front in World War One. While the antagonists in this work also tried to change history by staging a peace summit between the Tsar and the Kaiser on the Eastern Front, and an attempt to eliminate Star Trek Producer Gene Coon (not Roddenberry) when he was a child, the pebble hitting the stream theory with Freund was fascinating. If you get rid of Freund, there is perhaps no 1931 Dracula or 1932 The Mummy. I Love Lucy may not become a success because his cinematography skills were not there. Finally, if there is no I Love Lucy, there is probably no Desilu Studios that helped oversee the creation of Twilight Zone, Star Trek, and Mission Impossible. Imagine the possible changes to history, especially science and technological, if those movies or shows did not exist.

**How has your background as a social studies teacher and principal influenced your writing?**

A great deal. Without my background as an educator, there is no Jigsaw Universe. Many of the books are based in historical settings I learned about. The origin of the characters from Renaissance Academy are inspired by the twenty years I had my own charter school in the East Valley in Arizona.

I also want to take a moment and thank my wife, Dr. Gwyneth Gordon. While my background as an educator and sci-fi horror fan helped inspire the creation of the books, it is the support and encouragement of my wife that keeps me going in the creative process.

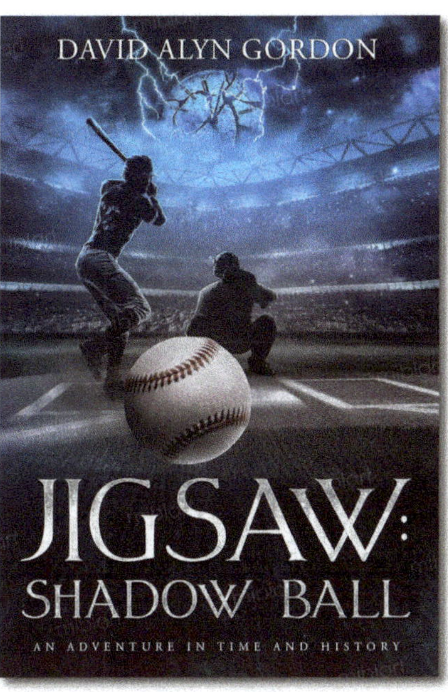


David Alyn Gordon's *Jigsaw: Shadow Ball* blends time travel, history, and social justice as Temporal Guardians Francesca and Noah battle Global Harmony's attempt to erase baseball's racial integration. With history at stake, they must protect legends Rube Foster and Larry Doby before the past—and the fight for justice—is lost forever.

**What advice would you offer to aspiring authors looking to write in the genres of science fiction and historical fiction?**

Never Give Up! If you want it enough, there is nothing more satisfying, outside family and friends, than creating a book that gets published.

Always research and outline before you write. That does not mean the story may not change but you need to be organized before writing the first sentence.

Get a good cover artist that will hook the reader into looking at your book.

Get good beta readers and a line editor. You may think what you have is perfect or near to it but I cannot tell you how many times I have written something and I say 'This is it' and then a beta reader or line editor points out something that I never thought of.

It is a probably going to be a long road to make money. Persevere. Put yourself out there at book events. Do digital ads on a budget you can afford. Network with fellow writers. Develop a marketing plan. These are all parts of being a successful writer too.

# Blending Fact, Fiction, and Imagination

Award-winning author Deanna Bussadori shares her creative journey, highlights the power of sibling bonds, reflects on multicultural influences, and discusses her commitment to inspiring young readers and giving back to communities.

# DEANNA BUSSADORI

## INSPIRES YOUNG MINDS WITH HER AWARD-WINNING STORIES OF SIBLING BONDS AND KINDNESS

Editor's Desk I London

"Watching my son naturally step into the role of a mentor for his younger sister inspired the Super Big Brother series."

Deanna Bussadori's enchanting ability to weave heartfelt themes with the lively cadence of rhyme has earned her a cherished place in the world of children's literature. With every turn of the page, her stories captivate the imaginations of young readers while gently imparting timeless values of kindness, resilience, and familial bonds. Her celebrated *Super Big Brother* series invites us into a world where sibling relationships are celebrated and shaped by vibrant characters and relatable milestones—a world inspired by her own family's journey.

An author whose pen flows effortlessly with poetic grace, Deanna draws from a mosaic of life experiences—her South African upbringing, her Greek heritage, and the courage it takes to adapt to new beginnings across the globe. Her books transcend boundaries, resonating with readers from diverse backgrounds. Whether penning stories that ease the transition of welcoming a new sibling or supporting charitable causes close to her heart, Deanna envisions a literary legacy that both uplifts and connects.

In this interview, Deanna Bussadori shares profound insights into her creative process, influences, and altruistic efforts as she continues to redefine how children's literature can shape lives. Join us in celebrating this award-winning author who marries storytelling with purpose, generosity, and an unmistakable love for her craft.

### What inspired you to create the *"Super Big Brother"* series, and how did you develop the themes of sibling bonds?

My debut book, Super Big Brother: Finding Your Hero, was inspired by my two children. Watching my son naturally step into the role of a mentor for his younger sister—who looked up to him as her hero—deepened my appreciation for their growing sibling bond. This connection inspired me to create stories that reflect the different stages of childhood and the unique relationship between siblings.

Their acts of kindness and the special growing milestones they shared became the foundation for my sibling series, weaving in themes of emotional growth, empathy, and support which inspired the creation of *Super Big Brother: The Big Brave School Day* and *Super Big Brother: New Baby Surprise for Super Big Sister.* I wanted to write stories that encourage children to be kind, help one another, and embrace the power of family bonds.

### Could you share the journey of writing in verse and how it shaped your storytelling approach?

Writing children's books in rhyme is where I feel most at home on this author journey—it's simply how my mind works. Since childhood, I've been drawn to the playful, rhythmic storytelling of Dr. Seuss, whose books were my favorites. Their catchy verses, vibrant illustrations, and fun style made them an engaging read, encouraging me to read them repeatedly. That love for poetry and rhyme has stayed with me, and it's one of the biggest reasons I enjoy writing in rhyme today.

### How does your cultural upbringing in South Africa and your Greek heritage influence your writing?

Growing up in South Africa in a Greek family with two siblings, I was always surrounded by loved ones—family and friends gathered around food, the outdoors, sunshine, the beach, and lively get-togethers. Our home was always open, with visitors coming and going, and these memories created a deep sense of connection that have influenced and shaped my writing.

> Deanna Bussadori masterfully blends creativity, heartfelt themes, and poetic charm to craft meaningful, award-winning stories that inspire children worldwide.

I believe it's important to encourage both single children and siblings to build strong family bonds, especially in today's fast-paced world, where it's easy to lose sight of the value of family roots and culture.

### What motivated your decision to donate your books to organisations like REACH-A-Child and Hindis Libraries, and how has this impacted you as an author?

As an author, I am committed to giving back and making sure children are supported with opportunities to read books. By donating books, I can support charities and share the gift of reading with more children. Organizations like REACH-A-Child and Hindi's Libraries are just a couple I've partnered with.

Recently, I donated my books to schools and libraries in Los Angeles who have been affected by the recent wildfires, to help rebuild their collections destroyed in the fires and in so doing, continue to inspire young readers. Donating not only expands reach and visibility for me as an author but more importantly helps build stronger communities.

### What were some of the challenges and joys you experienced while living in different countries, and how did these experiences influence your creativity?

Rebuilding your life multiple times when moving to different countries is one of the biggest challenges. Leaving behind extended family, friends, and familiar surroundings is never an easy decision and comes with additional difficulties and uncertainties. It requires resilience, determination, and a strong family effort.

Through these experiences, I've learned the importance of perseverance, facing challenges head-on, finding solutions, and having the courage to adapt. Believing in myself and my decisions have been crucial lessons, shaping not only my creativity in writing but also my resilience to keep moving forward.

In addition, the joy of watching my family grow, making new friendships, embracing new cultures, and experiencing different ways of life has been incredibly rewarding. These experiences have naturally woven themselves into my stories, adding depth, emotion, and a universal sense of connection.

### Can you tell us more about the process behind designing the award-winning cover for *"Super Big Brother: Finding Your Hero"*?

Designing an award-winning book cover is a thoughtful and collaborative process that blends creativity, market appeal, and storytelling. It begins with understanding the essence of the book—its themes, emotions, and target audience. My goal is always to create a visually striking design that not only grabs attention but also conveys the heart of the story in a single image.

I worked closely with a talented illustrator at Blueberry Illustrations, determining key elements that would make the cover stand out while staying true to the book's message. We explored different color palettes, typography, and compositions to find the perfect balance of eye-catching appeal to create something that would resonate with both children and parents.

Winning the Cover-of-the-Month AllAuthor award in June 2023 for Super Big Brother: Finding Your Hero was an incredible honor, reaffirming that a well-crafted design can enhance the reading experience and draw more readers into the story.

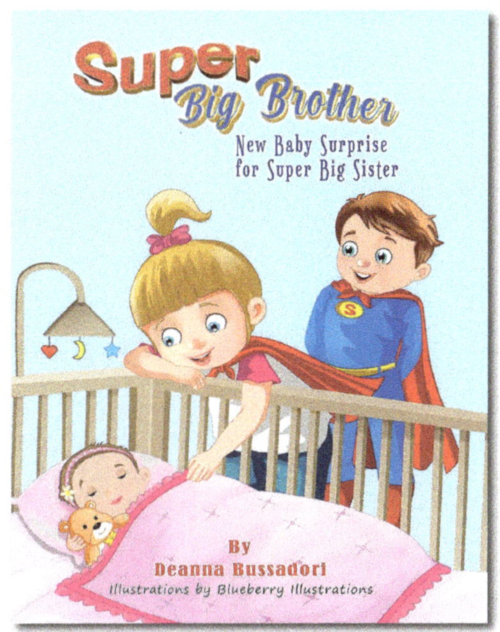


> *Super Big Brother: New Baby Surprise for Super Big Sister* by Deanna Bussadori is a charming story about Lulu coping with the arrival of a new sibling. Guided by Super Sam, she learns kindness, responsibility, and empathy. With engaging illustrations and positive messages, this book is a delightful read for young children.

### How do you balance crafting engaging stories for children while also imparting valuable lessons and themes?

Balancing engaging storytelling with meaningful lessons requires a blend of creativity, relatability, and subtle teaching. Rather than trying to teach a lesson, I subtly add valuable themes—such as kindness, bravery, and teamwork—naturally into the narrative.

Using rhyme and relatable experiences helps keep young readers engaged while allowing them to absorb positive messages, which aims to leave a lasting, meaningful impression.

### What advice would you give to aspiring authors looking to write meaningful and impactful children's books?

Don't overthink—just take action! Do your research, and if you have a story to tell, tell it. Passion is key; without passion, creating something meaningful can feel like an uphill battle. While inspiration may come and go, if you keep returning to an idea, that's a sign your passion is real. Don't let self-doubt hold you back—it's nothing but a distraction that keeps you from moving forward. Have a plan, stay committed, and follow through.

The Art of Writing and the Power of Love

# BARBARA AVON

## A JOURNEY OF LOVE, HORROR AND IMAGINATION

In October of 2022, "Revived" was chosen as "Horror Book of the Year" by the "Feed My Reads" community, and in February of 2025, "Sultry Is the Night", received the Literary Titan Gold Medal Award for Fiction.

Barbara Avon reflects on her writing journey, her diverse genres, and the profound themes of love and horror found in her award-winning novels.

as told to Dan Peters

Barbara Avon graces the cover of this issue of Reader's House, a testament to her remarkable contributions to contemporary literature. As an award-winning multi-genre author, Barbara has captivated readers with her imaginative storytelling, deftly navigating the realms of romance, horror, mystery, and beyond. Her writing journey began in the quiet recesses of her imagination as a young girl in the Niagara Falls Region, blossoming into a prolific career that has seen her achieve critical acclaim and recognition within the literary community.

Her works, including the award-winning "*Revived*" and "*Sultry Is the Night,*" showcase a unique blend of complexity and emotion that resonates deeply with readers. Barbara's exploration of themes such as love, loss, and the human experience invites us into a world where the lines between beauty and horror are artfully blurred. Her ability to breathe life into her characters, particularly her compelling male protagonists, highlights her skill as a storyteller, earning her accolades that celebrate her distinct voice.

In this insightful interview, readers will gain a glimpse into Barbara's writing process, her inspirations, and her unwavering belief in the magic of storytelling. As she shares her journey of self-publishing and her hopes for the legacy her works will leave behind, it becomes evident that Barbara Avon is not just a writer but a conjuror of emotions who believes in the transformative power of love and the written word. Join us as we delve into the mind of this extraordinary author, whose pen captures the essence of both joy and darkness, revealing the haunting beauty that resides in every tale she tells.

**Can you share more about the moment you decided to pursue writing seriously after your Grade 9 English teacher's encouragement? What impact did that have on your career?**

Most people feel "a calling". Whether they are drawn to the arts, a trade, or are

**Continued** *on page 42*

"Barbara Avon, a trailblazer in multi-genre literature, capturing hearts and minds with her enchanting narratives and compelling characters.

**Continued** *from page 40*

*"Owl Eyes Motel"* by Barbara Avon is a captivating journey through the eerie and atmospheric world of a quirky motel. Set in 1985, each room unveils a haunting story that keeps readers enthralled. Avon's writing is rich with vivid imagery and clever storytelling, inviting us to explore the mysteries of life and death. A must-read for fans of supernatural fiction!

> *"Love is the most remarkable magic - even in horror."*

business-minded, it's what shapes them as a person. Life for me evolved in a normal fashion: University, part-time jobs, a career in administration. It was until I was in my 30s and after a significant breakup that I decided to put pen to paper and write my first novel, "My Love is Deep". When my engagement ended, I had time on my hands and used that time to finally pursue the dream that had been brewing inside of me since Grade 9. Although I set that novel aside for many more years, it marked the beginning of this incredible journey. My first protagonist, Peter Travis, will always be a part of me.

**What draws you to explore such a wide range of genres, and do you have a favorite?**

One simple word can inspire many ideas. I can transform the word "horizon" into something romantic, or even horrific. Horror is my favourite genre to write. Life can be horrific. Exploring the human psyche is fascinating. As a storyteller, it's inherent in me to explore all genres.

**Could you describe your writing process? Do you have any specific rituals or routines when starting a new book?**

I don't practice any specific rituals per se, although unlike some of my peers, I do prefer to write in a quiet setting. However, I always decide on my title before I start writing. Next, I create my cover. Both those things inspire the rest of the story. I also edit as I write. I don't like to leave "bad words" behind, which means that I don't write several drafts.

**How do you develop your characters? Do you find that your characters take on a life of their own as the story progresses?**

They do take on a life of their own. I am instinctively drawn to writing male characters and I find it easy and satisfying to do so. I've had readers over the years tell me that had they not known I am a female author, they would have guessed that I was male since my male characters are written realistically. All my characters are as real to me as the flesh and blood person sitting next to me. They also reside somewhere inside of me.

**What messages or themes do you hope readers take away from your stories?**

I used this as my brand and in my advertising campaigns when I first started this journey, but it still rings true today: "Love is the most remarkable magic - even in horror." I suppose it's the hopeless romantic in me - the person who believes, and has always believed – that love can conquer all. There's a scene of dialogue in my first book that sums this up. The gist is, if someone is on their deathbed, they won't remember their first job, or care how much money is in their bank account. They will only want someone who loves them to be there to hold their hand.

> *"I believe in magic. Books are magic. Love is the most remarkable magic."*

**Can you elaborate on what you mean by horror being "hauntingly beautiful" to you as a writer?**

This is where the theme of love comes in. If love is all that matters in life, then there's a lot more at stake when two lovers are trapped in a horror story. By definition, a romance ends happily. That's not the case when it comes to horror. Can a tragic ending be beautiful? Death is a part of life. Love is a part of life. A horror story can be "hauntingly beautiful". There are, of course, different types of horror stories. Romantic love is not a theme in a slasher-type of horror, but my horror stories are categorized under Psychological Horror. Love is always a theme.

**How did it feel to receive recognition like the Literary Titan Gold Medal Award for "Sultry Is the Night"?**

As an author, I strive to write stories that touch readers in some way, shape, or form. "Sultry Is the Night" is one of my personal favourites. I feel honoured that the story received such high praise. Authors often refer to their books as their "babies". Just as a parent is proud when their child receives a prestigious award and recognition, I also feel proud.

**Which of your works do you envision as a movie, and why?**

By using colourful descriptions and realistic dialogue, I think all my books read like movies. "Sacrilege", my psychological horror, is set in 1985 and would be low budget since most of the action takes place in a boarding house. I envision someone like Patrick Wilson (The Conjuring) playing wayward priest Cris Corelli. Seeing my stories come to life on the big screen is my next big dream.

**Can you share more about your journey into self-publishing? What challenges did you face, and how did you overcome them?**

I always knew that I wanted to be in control of every aspect from writing, editing, cover design, and marketing. I never queried and preferred to retain creative control. Basically,

> *"My first protagonist, Peter Travis, will always be a part of me."*

I run my own business as an author. I am my own publisher. The biggest challenge is marketing and being seen in a sea of other authors. Being passionate means never giving up.

**How does cooking influence your creativity or writing process?**

One doesn't influence the other. I simply share my love of cooking in a fictional sense. My food descriptions almost read like recipes which is a bonus for any reader who is interested in cooking, and especially Italian food. I love that both writing and cooking are the same. Both require a pinch of imagination, an ounce of patience, and whole lot of love.

**What legacy do you hope to leave behind through your writing, and how do you want to be remembered as an author?**

I was never able to be a mother. My books are my legacy. Within them, a reader can catch glimpses of me and who I am (or who I was). In the end, the stories are what matter, and they will be like time capsules, of sorts. Once a reader opens one of my books, my entire life – from my Italian roots to my fiercely independent nature – can be read between the lines.

## BARBARA AVON

Barbara Avon grew up Italian in the Niagara Falls Region and attended Notre Dame High School, and then Brock University. In 1999, she moved to Ottawa to pursue work and has worked for two major Ottawa area magazines. Being a shy kid in school, she created stories in her head, and when her Grade 9 English teacher awarded one of her short stories an A +, she knew that she would one day write a novel.

Avon is a multi-genre author. She's written Romance, Romantic Thrillers, Time Travel, Mystery, Horror, and Paranormal Romance. Her work appears in various anthologies including Steering 23 Publications, Storytime for Grownups, and Beyond the Levee. In October of 2022, "Revived" was chosen as "Horror Book of the Year" by the "Feed My Reads" community, and in February of 2025, "Sultry Is the Night", received the Literary Titan Gold Medal Award for Fiction.

When she's not writing, she's experimenting in the kitchen, reading, watching 1980s movies, and working on her next novel. Avon has quoted: I believe in magic. Books are magic. Love is the most remarkable magic.

# Award-Winning Author on Wisdom, Vision, and Fulfilment

Dr Ketan Kulkarni discusses blending ancient wisdom with science, tackling burnout in medicine, crafting impactful books, and guiding others toward authentic success, purpose, and inner transformation through storytelling and coaching.

# DR KETAN KULKARNI

## SOARING TO NEW HEIGHTS

Editor's Desk I London

Dr Ketan Kulkarni stands as a remarkable figure whose unwavering commitment to excellence transcends the domains of medicine, education, and personal development. As a paediatrician and a blood disorder and cancer specialist, his contributions over the past two decades have been nothing short of revolutionary. With more than 350 original studies published in leading medical journals, Dr Kulkarni has not only enhanced the standard of care for childhood cancer patients but has also advocated for their wellbeing on a global scale. His passion for mentorship and education is reflected in his nurturing of over a thousand students, guiding them towards their own paths of success.

Beyond his medical achievements, Dr Kulkarni is an embodiment of the transformative power of blending ancient wisdom with modern scientific principles. His internationally acclaimed books, including *The Legendary Quest* and *Soar: A Soul's Quest*, explore profound themes of success, fulfilment, and self-discovery. These works offer readers a unique perspective that harmonises traditional Indian philosophies with contemporary insights, making essential contributions to the self-help genre. His literary prowess resonates deeply with audiences around the world, garnering multiple international accolades and rave reviews.

Dr Kulkarni's innovative spirit extends to his entrepreneurial ventures, where he embodies a commitment to sustainability and social responsibility. His initiatives in providing quality housing and ethical education reflect his deep-seated belief in uplifting the underserved segments of society. Additionally, his efforts to combat burnout within the medical profession through coaching and wellness programs demonstrate his holistic approach to healthcare—a testament to his understanding that personal wellbeing is crucial for effective service in medicine.

"I truly believe that authenticity, purpose and meaning are key for success and fulfilment." - Ketan Kulkarni

In this interview, Dr Ketan Kulkarni shares invaluable insights into his journey, the inspiration behind his writing, and his vision for a more fulfilling life. His articulate responses illuminate the paths to authenticity and purpose, making this dialogue not just an exploration of his works, but a guide for anyone seeking to navigate the complexities of modern existence. Readers will find in Dr Kulkarni's words both encouragement and a call to action to embark on their own quests for meaning and success.

### What inspired you to blend ancient wisdom with modern science in your book *"The Legendary Quest"*?

While the words success and fulfilment are used extremely frequently, current global data suggests an extremely high levels of personal and professional burnout, stress, exhaustion, mental illness epidemic. A lot of work and life satisfaction data doesn't suggest people experience authentic fulfilment, happiness and success regardless of what they achieve, and how hard or smart they work! Happiness and joy seem to be fleeting and limited to brief moments such as holidays, certain life events, and sporadic circumstances. The result is that individuals believe these states are normal and expected! That they must exist! And that life is but a struggle, not a wonderful journey.

We wrote "The Legendary quest" as a life changing guidebook in an attempt to address this extremely important issue at the very core of our human existence and experience!

> Dr Kulkarni is a rare and inspiring force, blending intellect, compassion, and creativity to uplift minds and transform countless lives.

We have written this book to answer these questions, and because we could not find a comprehensive resource that addressed these concerns in a simple, digestible format using evidence-based resources. We deeply explored both ancient wisdom and modern science. This book is our sincere attempt to present our deliberations, analysis, experience and investigations into a variety of these fields and to describe them in a comprehensive and unified manner. The book has been widely cited and won the BIBA 2023 best self-help book award.

### How has your background as a physician influenced your approach to coaching and self-help?

Wellness and wellbeing are truly at the forefront of challenges in medicine and for medical workforce. A healthy workforce is a necessity to fulfil the need of ever-increasing complexity of healthcare and patient needs. Financial awareness is a key aspect too with a lot of work is needed in the area.

My own personal experience with clinical work, academic, extensive publishing and administration and leadership and entrepreneurship has provided me with a deep insight into these issues. Additionally, my leadership and coaching training and experience has refined my skillset further as we developed our own original coaching models and exercises. Many of these are published in the Legendary Quest.

Through these I am able to bring a high level of awareness to my coaching practice and act as a strong transforming catalyst in anyone's journey towards success and fulfilment.

### Could you share some of the most impactful life lessons you've learned during your journey of self-discovery?

I truly believe that authenticity, purpose and meaning are key for success and fulfilment. Additionally, regardless of their current circumstances, anyone can access and work towards authentic success if they put in the right effort.

### How did the concept of *"Soar: A Soul's Quest"* come to life, and what message do you hope it conveys to readers?

I truly believe that there's a Soar in some capacity in all of us. All of us are capable of living the best possible lives we can and becoming the best versions of ourselves. So, the idea of Soar came from the verb soar.

Soar: A soul's quest is an inspirational fable of a young eagle who goes on an epic journey of self-realization and personal growth. Questions the way we live our lives. At its heart, Soar is a quest for excellence, self-improvement, personal mastery, wrapped in a beautiful and inspiring fable.

At the beginning of the story, Soar is forced to abandon everything that is familiar to him, and branch out into the unknown alone, on what becomes an epic journey of discovery and transformation. Soar is primarily a tale of self-awareness, and involves an often trying and testing, but ultimately rewarding, journey.

So far Soar has received 5 international awards and over 60 5-star reviews on variety of platforms.

> *Soar: A Soul's Quest* follows a young eagle's journey of self-discovery and spiritual growth. Through encounters with wise creatures, Soar learns life-changing lessons about authenticity and purpose. This inspiring fable offers profound insights for readers of all ages, encouraging reflection and a deeper connection to one's true self.

### What challenges did you face while balancing your career as a physician with your entrepreneurial ventures?

Time and task management have certainly been key. Ensuring that I appropriately care for my patients was essential to me as was balancing my family and personal life and responsibility.

I have realized that unless you have a passion for something and the zeal to make a difference, your entrepreneurial journey is less likely to be successful. One needs to bring their authentic heart and soul to embark this journey and to make a meaningful impact.

### How do you approach the topic of burnout, particularly within the medical profession, and how can individuals overcome it?

Given the magnitude of the issue, I find that the best way to discuss the topic of burnout is through being vulnerable and sharing personal journey. This makes a huge impact. It immediately connects people, and they start seeing and validating their own experience which is often similar in many ways.

We are also doing a lot of collective work to bring the topic of burnout to the forefront of all discussions in clinical medicine and academia. This is essential to raise awareness of the issue.

It is only through open communication, transparency, accountability, collective work, and mentorship and coaching that medical community can face the issue of burnout. At individual level, everyone needs to understand their core values, what's meaningful to them at personal level and embark on their own Legendary Quest!

### What advice would you give to other authors looking to make a meaningful impact with their writing and connect with a wide audience?

I truly believe that there is no magic formula and certainly no shortcut. One must take action, put yourself out there, be visible, share your story, seek and accept feedback, be open to change, be adaptable, keep trying and keep sharing. Certainly, you will find your tribe and make a meaningful impact.

Failure isn't when you don't succeed, its only when you give up!

# Awakening Creativity and Inner Leadership

Elaine Patterson discusses the vital role of reflection in leadership and life, sharing insights from her books on creativity, inner wisdom, and finding joy, authenticity and compassion in modern times.

# ELAINE PATTERSON

## REFLECTS ON THE POWER OF CREATIVE REFLECTION AND THE ART OF COMING HOME TO OURSELVES

"People cannot be commanded to be more reflective — the preconditions and permissions must be set."

Editor's Desk I London

Elaine Patterson's profound commitment to fostering creativity and reflection makes her a truly inspirational figure in contemporary literature and coaching. As the founder of the Centre for Reflection and Creativity Ltd, she merges her passions for nature, the arts, and personal development, embodying the very principles she advocates in her works. Between the vibrant pulse of London and the serene expanses of the Lake District, Elaine channels her experiences into her writing, design, and creative coaching, aiming to awaken the beauty of the human spirit and nurture a kinder world.

Her innovative titles, such as "Reflect to Create! The Dance of Reflection for Creative Leadership, Supervision and Professional Practice" and "Homecomings ~ 52 Ways Back to Ourselves," encapsulate her philosophy that reflection is not merely an act of introspection but a vital practice that can lead to profound transformation. By challenging conventional notions of creativity and reflection, Elaine invites readers to embark on a journey of self-discovery and connection with their authentic selves.

In her collaboration with Karyn Prentice on "The Compass Rose - 8 Ways to Awake your Creativity and Re-Source your Life," she provides illuminating pathways for readers to reclaim their innate creativity. Elaine's insights into reflective practice emphasise the essential role it plays in leadership and personal growth, offering a refreshing perspective that resonates across diverse cultural landscapes.

This interview offers a rare glimpse into the mind of an author whose work is not only a source of inspiration but also a practical guide for creating a life rich in creativity and reflection. We are honoured to share her thoughts and experiences with our readers, as they undoubtedly hold the potential to spark transformation in both personal and professional realms.

**How did your background in executive coaching and coaching supervision influence the development of your book "Reflect to Create! The Dance of Reflection for Creative Leadership, Supervision and Professional Practice"?**

I came to see that reflection is THE meta capacity for insight, learning and change. I see it as a necessity - not a luxury - to all that we do to be the best that we can be.

I wanted to challenge the dreary plodding image that reflection often has when it is squeezed into the margins in the workplace and in professional practice.

I want to show it was possible to make the processes of creative reflection fun, awakening, enlivening and empowering from which profound transformational change can be birthed. My MA research also proved to me that reflection is an act of creativity whether it be to stop what is no longer working, to improve what already exists and to create anew.

And that this speaks to our innate desire as human beings which we all share which is to continually learn and to endlessly create.

**Could you elaborate on the concept of 'reflective practice' and its significance in creative leadership, as discussed in your work?**

As Einstein famously said 'problems cannot be solved from the consciousness which created them'. Doing more of the same is no longer enough. 'Reflective practice' is an umbrella term for the regular discipline of reflection which can take many forms – but most importantly can put us in touch with the seeds of the new – of what is wanting to emerge if we can learnt to become still, pay exquisite attention and truly listen.

> Elaine Patterson inspires with depth and heart, offering soulful guidance that uplifts creativity, fosters reflection, and transforms both life and leadership.

Reflective practice takes many forms including journaling, meditative walking, crafting, art, poetry, music coaching and supervision and the key is to find the menu that works for us.

I believe that it is the ethical duty of anyone who works with people to have a regular reflective practice where they can push the pause button and reflect deeply on what is happening within them and around them. Because who you are is how you work.

**In "Homecomings ~ 52 Ways Back to Ourselves," you offer reflective soliloquies and creative resources. How do you envision these aiding individuals in reconnecting with their authentic selves?**

I wanted to explore what it means to belong and how we can come home to ourselves as a foundational practice for our times. The jewel of great price is remembering to know ourselves and to come home to ourselves before we can act in the world with compassion, authenticity and integrity. I feel that this has never been more important and necessary if we are to live in the midst of all that is happening within us and in the world with joy, beauty, generosity, compassion, courage, kindness, wonder, reciprocity, wisdom and grace.

The 52 reflective soliloquies and supporting resources are designed to invite readers into their own reflections.

And I believe that finding our way back to ourselves can be as frustrating and elusive as it is enriching – as we try to catch the threads of wisdom that life is trying to show us. It is a continual process of feeling lost and found, of arrival and departure, of disconnecting and re-connecting and of forgetting and remembering. The destination is always moving and can never feel complete because we are already changed in our setting off. As we learn to hold these frontiers for ourselves, our understanding of life and living deepens with each encounter.

I hope that this book will become Readers' own companion self-care kit which feels relevant and contemporary each and every time that they open it.

**As co-founder of PattersonPrenticeDesigns, how do you integrate your passion for the arts, nature, and creativity into your professional practice?**

With my partner Karyn Prentice in PattersonPrenticeDesigns our abiding friendship and our shared love of the arts, nature and creativity is our starting point and our connecting point from which everything else is birthed and infused. Our passions lift our work from being ordinary to being soulful and extraordinary in a world which needs both radical hope and loving kindness in spades!

**Your book with Karyn Prentice "The Compass Rose - 8 Ways to Awake your Creativity and Re-Source your Life" introduces eight cardinal points as touchstones for creativity. Could you share how these points guide individuals in reclaiming their innate creativity?**

We believe that we are all innately creative – but we also fully understand how our creativity can get educated out of us or lost in the busyness of our 'to do' lists'. Every choice we make can be creative – from what we choose to wear designing a new product - if want to make it so! We believe that our creativity is our soul speaking through us in the world.

We therefore designed the eight cardinal points as touchstones where readers can explore ways to claim (or reclaim) their innate creativity. The focus is on what we call the 'work before the work' – of designing through the eight cardinal points the spaces, places, activities and people who can both support, inspire and nourish our own creativity – which of course will be different for each of us.

Reflecting on your extensive experience in executive coaching, what are the most common challenges leaders face when attempting to incorporate reflective practices into their routines?

I feel that the most important challenge is leaders is failing to appreciate what reflective practices

> *Homecomings: 52 Ways Back to Ourselves* by Elaine Patterson is a reflective collection of soliloquies and journaling prompts encouraging readers to reconnect with themselves. Born from lockdown journaling, it invites deep introspection, creativity, and self-compassion, offering a heart-based path to inner belonging, resilience, and personal transformation.

can do for them – and their teams - to open up different kinds of learning conversations be even more brilliant. They just need to be prioritised. And it starts with the leaders who can role model this approach within their own teams and organisations. People cannot be commanded to be more reflective. The preconditions and the permissions need to be set so that it is seen as a necessity and not a designer luxury. And to remove the guilt and associations attached to reflecting rather than being seen to be endlessly busy.

**Considering your international work, how do cultural differences influence the application of reflective practices in leadership across various regions?**

We are all human and therefore I believe that we all love to learn. The key therefore is for each person whatever their background is finding what works uniquely for them and their own context.

**What advice would you offer to fellow authors aiming to blend creative reflection with professional development in their writings?**

Just try it! Do what works for you! Enjoy yourself! Allow yourself to be amazed and delighted!

## WISHES ARE FREE

### *by Diana Mercedes Howell*

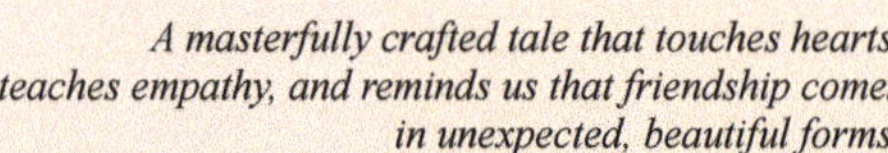

*A masterfully crafted tale that touches hearts, teaches empathy, and reminds us that friendship comes in unexpected, beautiful forms.*

*Cover by Moran Reudor*

*Wishes Are Free* is a heartwarming tale that masterfully captures the emotional landscape of childhood friendship, loss, and healing. Diana Mercedes Howell has crafted a touching narrative that resonates with both young readers and adults alike.

The story centres on ten-year-old Rose O'Reilly, who faces the devastating departure of her best friend Linney. Through her special Sunday kitchen chats with her recently widowed grandfather, Rose embarks on a journey of emotional growth and discovery. The parallel between Rose's loss of her friend and Grandpa's loss of his wife creates a beautiful symmetry that adds depth to their relationship.

Howell's writing style is refreshingly authentic, capturing the voice of a ten-year-old with remarkable accuracy whilst maintaining a sophisticated emotional undertone. The introduction of diverse characters, including a boy with cerebral palsy and a classmate dealing with troubling circumstances at home, adds layers of complexity to the narrative without overwhelming young readers.

The book excels in teaching valuable lessons about friendship, empathy, and resilience without being preachy. The metaphor of wishes being free serves as a powerful reminder that hope costs nothing but can yield remarkable results.

The cover illustration by Moran Reudor complement the story beautifully, enhancing the emotional resonance of key moments throughout the book.

This award-winning book is particularly suited for children aged 8-12, but its universal themes of love, loss, and friendship will touch readers of all ages. It's no surprise that it has garnered multiple accolades, including the Bronze Medal in Readers' Favorite Children's Coming of Age Category.

A truly memorable read that handles complex emotions with grace and sensitivity.

## CAGED

### *by CC Robinson*

*A gripping, fast-paced dystopian sequel with high stakes, compelling characters, and relentless tension—Caged keeps readers hooked from start to finish.*

Caged, the second instalment in CC Robinson's *Divided* series, is a gripping YA dystopian novel that keeps readers on edge from start to finish. Picking up where *Divided* left off, we find protagonist Rose in an even more dire situation—stripped of her freedom, trapped in a literal prison, and cut off from those who once stood by her side.

Robinson crafts a tense, claustrophobic atmosphere that mirrors Rose's predicament, making every chapter pulse with urgency. The stakes are higher than ever, as Rose not only fights for her own survival but also for the future of her city. Her journey from helpless captive to determined fighter is compelling, showcasing resilience and the power of hope in the face of tyranny.

One of the novel's greatest strengths is its pacing. The action never falters, and as Rose unravels the sinister schemes of her captors, the tension builds masterfully. The story is interwoven with moments of reflection and character growth, ensuring that it's not just about high-stakes action but also about the emotional depth of its heroine.

Readers who enjoyed *Divergent or The Giver* will appreciate the familiar dystopian themes, yet *Caged* maintains its own unique identity. With a well-developed world, gripping suspense, and a protagonist worth rooting for, this sequel solidifies the *Divided* series as a must-read for fans of the genre.

An electrifying read that delivers both heart and adrenaline—Robinson does not disappoint.

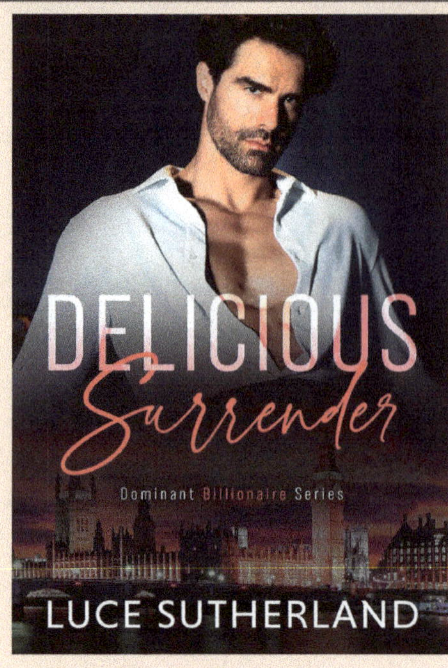


## DELICIOUS SURRENDER

### *by Luce Sutherland*

*Intensely passionate, thrillingly suspenseful, and irresistibly steamy—Delicious Surrender delivers fiery chemistry, gripping tension, and a deeply satisfying romance.*

Luce Sutherland delivers a steamy, high-stakes romance in *Delicious Surrender*, the first instalment of the *Dominant Billionaire Series*. With a tantalising mix of power play, sizzling chemistry, and emotional depth, this novel is an enticing read for fans of the grumpy-sunshine trope.

Brynne Larimore, an independent and headstrong writer, finds herself entangled in the dark allure of Club Dominus, a world ruled by the icy and domineering Gage MacLeod. Their dynamic is electric—Brynne's defiance sparks fire against Gage's relentless control, making for an intoxicating push-and-pull. The tension is palpable, with Sutherland masterfully balancing fiery exchanges with moments of raw vulnerability.

While the romance is undeniably steamy, what sets this book apart is its suspenseful undercurrent. The presence of a dangerous Russian club member adds an element of intrigue, forcing Gage to confront not only his protective instincts but also his own vulnerabilities. The stakes rise when betrayal threatens his business, pushing both characters to their limits.

Sutherland's writing is crisp and immersive, painting a vivid picture of London's elite club scene while delving into themes of trust, power, and emotional surrender. The pacing is tight, keeping the reader hooked through every twist and turn.

If you enjoy passionate, angst-ridden romances with dominant yet redeemable heroes, *Delicious Surrender* will not disappoint. The hard-fought happy ending is well-earned, making this a satisfying start to what promises to be a compelling series.

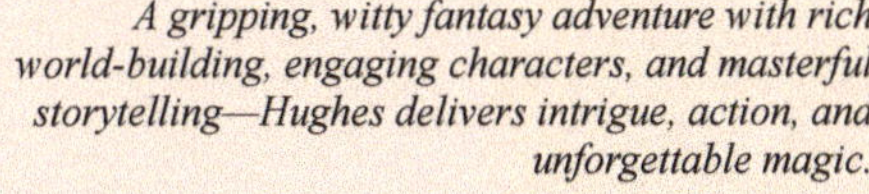

## HENCHMEN

*by Matthew Hughes*

*A gripping, witty fantasy adventure with rich world-building, engaging characters, and masterful storytelling—Hughes delivers intrigue, action, and unforgettable magic.*

Matthew Hughes' *Henchmen* is a gripping fantasy novel that blends adventure, intrigue, and a touch of dry humour into a thoroughly enjoyable read. Set in a world where even employment is dictated by a Duke's decree, the story follows Vunt, a gambler, and Oldo, a farm boy, as they stumble into a job that is both lucrative and deeply suspicious. Their new employer's shifty dealings soon propel them into a far greater and more dangerous world than they ever imagined.

The novel masterfully balances classic fantasy elements with a refreshing, character-driven narrative. Hughes excels in crafting protagonists who feel authentic—Vunt's cunning contrasts nicely with Oldo's naivety, making their dynamic both engaging and entertaining. As the pair are drawn into a web of espionage, wizardly schemes, and perilous travels, the plot unfolds with a steady momentum that keeps the pages turning.

Hughes' writing is rich yet accessible, reminiscent of classic adventure fantasy but with a modern wit that makes it stand out. The setting is immersive, with detailed world-building that never overwhelms the reader. The city of Olliphract, with its unpredictable thaumaturges, is a particularly fascinating backdrop.

For fans of fantasy that doesn't take itself too seriously yet delivers on action and intrigue, *Henchmen* is a must-read. Hughes proves once again that he is a master of weaving intelligent, well-paced storytelling with a unique voice. Highly recommended.

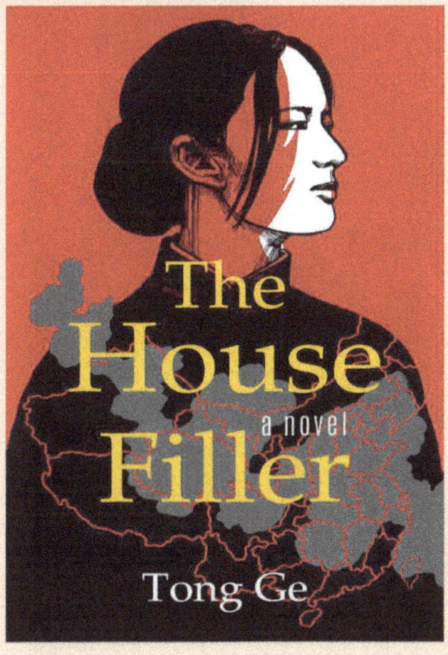


## THE HOUSE FILLER

*by Tong Ge*

*A beautifully written, emotionally powerful novel that captures resilience, love, and survival amidst the turmoil of war and political unrest.*

The House Filler is a deeply moving and richly layered novel that captures the personal cost of war and political upheaval through the eyes of a resilient woman, Golden Phoenix. Set against the backdrop of China's civil war and Japanese occupation, Tong Ge's narrative is both heart-wrenching and inspiring.

Golden Phoenix is a formidable protagonist. Following her husband's premature death, she is left to raise her children amidst chaos and uncertainty. Her struggle to preserve her family through famine, violence, and separation forms the emotional core of the novel. The most harrowing moments come during the Japanese occupation, where she and her adopted son face unimaginable suffering. Yet, through it all, her spirit never truly breaks.

Ge's prose is elegant and evocative, immersing the reader in both the beauty and brutality of 20th-century China. The historical detail is meticulously researched, giving the story a powerful sense of authenticity without ever feeling like a history lesson. Characters are vividly drawn, especially the twin daughters and the son who joins the Nationalist army, each of whom adds depth to the family's fractured portrait.

Ending in 1965, on the eve of the Cultural Revolution, the novel leaves readers with a haunting sense of what is still to come. *The House Filler* is not just a tale of survival—it's a tribute to maternal love, endurance, and the quiet strength required to hold a family together in the darkest of times.

Highly recommended for fans of historical fiction with emotional depth.

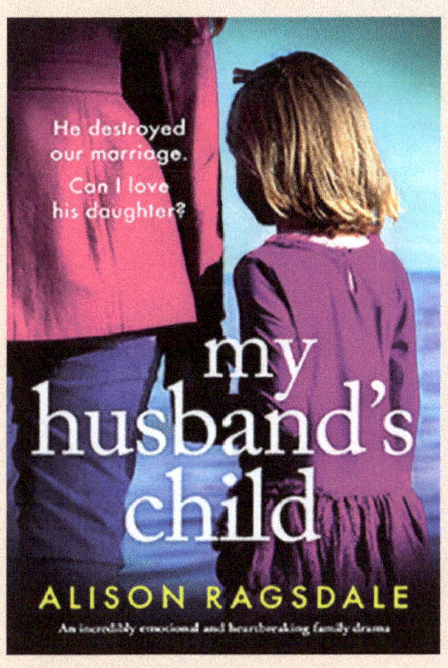


## MY HUSBAND'S CHILD

*by Alison Ragsdale*

*A beautifully written, emotionally gripping novel with vivid characters, heartfelt storytelling, and a captivating exploration of motherhood and sacrifice.*

Alison Ragsdale's *My Husband's Child* is a captivating and emotionally charged family drama that plunges readers into a complex web of love, trust, and heart-rending choices. From the moment a little girl appears at Cora's doorstep, clutching her baby brother's hand, with the haunting words, "Mummy said you'd look after me," the story grips you and doesn't let go.

Ragsdale paints a vivid portrait of a woman rebuilding her life after heartbreak, only to have it disrupted in the most unexpected and poignant way. The children's sudden arrival throws Cora into a situation fraught with mystery and emotional stakes. The narrative beautifully captures her struggles as she balances her growing bond with the children against the murky circumstances surrounding their abandonment. Themes of motherhood, sacrifice, and loyalty are explored with sensitivity, making every twist and revelation feel both authentic and startling.

The characters are richly developed, and Ragsdale's writing is evocative and engaging. As Cora navigates the conflicting accounts of her ex-husband and his wife, the tension is palpable, keeping you guessing about whom to trust. Although the novel is deeply emotional, it avoids descending into melodrama, maintaining a grounded and relatable perspective on the challenges of raising children thrust into an extraordinary situation.

Fans of compelling family dramas by authors like Kate Hewitt and Diane Chamberlain will find themselves enthralled. *My Husband's Child* is a beautifully crafted tale that lingers in your mind long after the final page. It's a must-read for anyone drawn to stories of resilience and the extraordinary power of love.

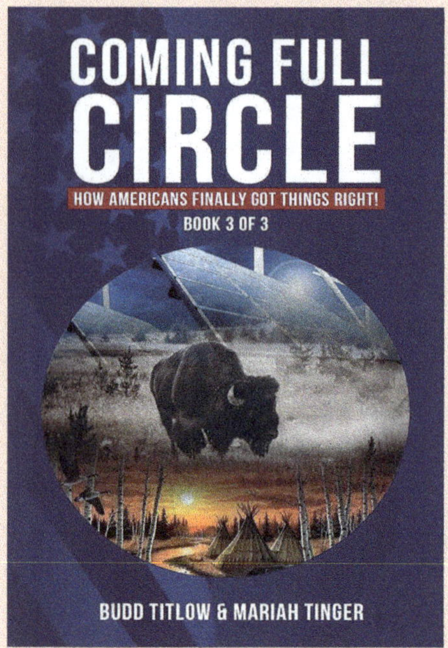


## COMING FULL CIRCLE

### *by Budd Titlow*

*A powerful, thought-provoking novel that masterfully blends history, environmental awareness, and human resilience—both captivating and deeply inspiring.*

Budd Titlow and Mariah Tinger deliver a compelling conclusion to their *Coming Full Circle* trilogy, a thought-provoking narrative that intertwines history, environmental consciousness, and the resilience of the human spirit. This final instalment builds upon the themes explored in the previous volumes, guiding readers through pivotal moments in American history while confronting the urgent question: can we learn from the past before it's too late?

Titlow, a wildlife biologist and wetlands scientist, brings his expertise to the forefront, crafting a narrative that is both educational and emotionally resonant. The novel follows a diverse set of characters whose stories reflect the evolving relationship between humans and nature. Their struggles and triumphs highlight the environmental and social issues that have shaped America, urging readers to reflect on the lessons history offers.

What makes *Coming Full Circle* stand out is its ability to blend fiction with pressing real-world concerns. The novel is not merely a historical recounting but a call to action, challenging readers to reconsider their role in the planet's future. Titlow and Tinger's storytelling is immersive, with vivid descriptions and well-researched details that bring each era to life.

For those who appreciate environmentally-conscious fiction with a historical and personal dimension, this book is a fitting and satisfying conclusion to an important series. A compelling read that both educates and inspires, *Coming Full Circle* is a timely reminder that history's lessons should not be ignored.

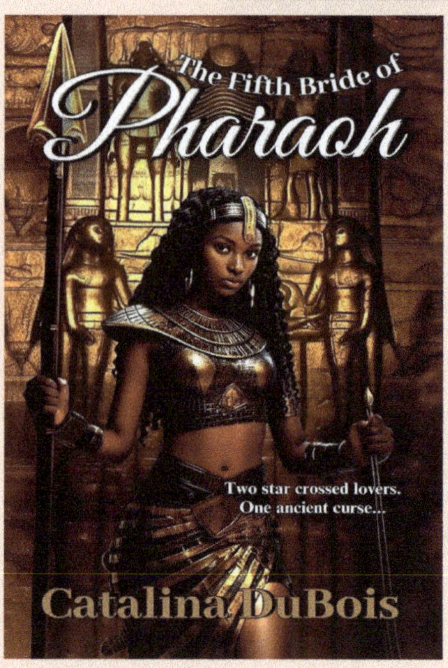


## THE FIFTH BRIDE OF PHARAOH

### *by Catalina DuBois*

*A beautifully written, emotionally gripping tale of love, sacrifice, and defiance set in a vividly immersive ancient Egyptian world. Captivating and unforgettable!*

Catalina DuBois delivers a compelling tale of forbidden love, duty, and defiance in *INFINITY: The Fifth Bride of Pharaoh*. Set against the grandeur of ancient Egypt, this novel blends romance and historical intrigue, drawing readers into the lives of its two star-crossed protagonists.

Sara, a Nubian princess, is bound by duty to become the fifth wife of the all-powerful Pharaoh. However, her heart gravitates towards Matthaios, a foreign slave who sees her as more than just a royal prize. Through richly descriptive prose, DuBois paints a world where power and privilege dictate fates, yet love dares to challenge the established order. Matthaios is a particularly intriguing character, torn between his loyalty as a servant and his growing affections for a woman he cannot claim. His perspective provides an emotional depth that makes their romance both compelling and tragic.

The novel excels in its atmospheric setting, vividly portraying courtly life, rituals, and the constraints placed upon women of the era. While the central romance is deeply engaging, some readers may find the pacing uneven, with moments of swift action followed by slower introspection. Nevertheless, the chemistry between Sara and Matthaios carries the story, making their struggle against societal expectations both poignant and memorable.

For lovers of historical romance, *INFINITY: The Fifth Bride of Pharaoh* offers a captivating escape into a world of passion, sacrifice, and defiance. It is a story that lingers long after the final page, leaving readers to ponder the true cost of love and freedom.

## REUNION BY THE LAKE

### *by James Gilbert*

*A poignant and deeply moving novel, Reunion by the Lake masterfully explores family, legacy, and the emotional weight of inheritance.*

James Gilbert's *Reunion by the Lake* is a poignant family drama that explores the weight of legacy, the complexities of familial bonds, and the struggle for closure in the face of impending loss. When Richard Collins gathers his three sons at their lakeside home to disclose his will before his death, he unknowingly sets off a storm of emotions, long-buried tensions, and bitter reckonings.

The novel masterfully captures the dynamics of a family shaped by Richard's dominance, as each son reacts in his own way to the looming reality of his father's mortality. Gilbert's writing is subtle yet powerful, weaving a narrative that is both intimate and unsettling. He delves into the fragile nature of relationships, showing how grief and inheritance can either tear people apart or force them to confront truths they've long avoided.

One of the novel's greatest strengths lies in its characterisation. The sons—each uniquely flawed and deeply affected by their upbringing—offer a compelling study in contrasts, and Grace, Richard's wife, provides a quietly resonant counterpoint to the family's turmoil. The setting of the lake house, with its serene yet isolating presence, mirrors the emotional undercurrents of the story.

While the pacing occasionally lags, particularly in its reflective moments, the emotional depth and realism of the novel make it a rewarding read. *Reunion by the Lake* is a thought-provoking exploration of family, regret, and the legacies we leave behind. An engaging and heartfelt novel for those who enjoy character-driven narratives.

## TWELVE PALOMINOS

*by Joe Kilgore*

*A thrilling, fast-paced detective novel with sharp writing, relentless action, and a compelling protagonist. Kilgore masterfully blends intrigue, danger, and suspense.*

Joe Kilgore's *Twelve Palominos* is a gripping, fast-paced detective novel that delivers action, intrigue, and a touch of old-school noir charm. In this latest instalment of the Brig Ellis series, Kilgore's sharp-witted private investigator is drawn into a case that begins as a simple acquisition and spirals into a treacherous game of survival.

Brig Ellis is hired by a wealthy industrialist to track down the last of twelve palomino miniatures once owned by China's last emperor. What should be a straightforward task soon plunges him into a whirlwind of danger, involving ruthless criminals, political adversaries, and a remorseless assassin. Kilgore keeps the tension high, layering the plot with twists and keeping the reader guessing at every turn. The enigmatic presence of the employer's daughter adds an element of uncertainty—both a potential ally and a liability.

Kilgore's writing is crisp and cinematic, evoking the feel of classic hardboiled detective fiction while injecting it with modern urgency. The action is relentless, and Ellis is a compelling lead—resourceful, tough, and wryly humorous. His encounters with kidnappers, spies, and killers make for exhilarating reading, and the global stakes give the novel a thrilling intensity.

While *Twelve Palominos* is the fifth book in the series, it stands well on its own. Fans of detective thrillers, espionage, and classic noir will find plenty to enjoy. Kilgore proves once again that Brig Ellis is a PI worth following—if he can stay alive.

## MACGREGOR'S FINAL BATTLE

*by Joe Clark*

*A beautifully written tale of love and resilience, this novel captivates readers with its emotional depth and relatable characters. Highly recommended!*

*MacGregor's Final Battle* by Joe Clark is a poignant exploration of life, love, and the inexorable passage of time. At its heart lies the story of Donald (Mac) MacGregor, a man confronting terminal brain cancer, who embarks on a final journey in an RV across the Lewis and Clark Trail. Along the way, he encounters Kate Graham, a nurse yearning for a change from her stagnant existence. Their whirlwind adventure unfolds against the backdrop of stunning landscapes, resonating with themes of hope and renewal.

Clark's writing is both evocative and insightful, skilfully intertwining the characters' emotional arcs with their physical journey. Mac and Kate, though fundamentally different, find solace in each other, allowing them to confront their fears and desires. Their connection is described with a tender authenticity that draws the reader in, making their struggles and triumphs feel deeply relatable.

The narrative balances moments of light-heartedness with profound emotional depth, creating a bittersweet ambience that lingers long after the final page. As fate intervenes in unexpected ways, readers are left contemplating the fragility of happiness and the importance of seizing life's fleeting moments.

Recommended for fans of romantic dramas and slice-of-life storytelling, *MacGregor's Final Battle* is an inspiring tale that underscores the resilience of the human spirit and the transformative power of love. Joe Clark has crafted a memorable odyssey that celebrates life's unpredictability, making it a must-read for those eager to embark on a journey of the heart.

## THE SPACE TRAVELLER'S LOVER

*by Omara Williams*

*A thrilling blend of romance and sci-fi, rich world-building, gripping tension, and unforgettable characters—an unmissable, heart-pounding interstellar adventure!*

Omara Williams' *The Space Traveller's* Lover is a captivating blend of fantasy and romance that transports readers into a world where dreams and reality intertwine. At its core, the narrative follows Erin, a protagonist haunted by mysterious dreams of a golden-uniformed soldier. This recurring dream sets the stage for a journey filled with emotional depth and imaginative exploration, where Erin's longing and emotional struggles come to life through vivid descriptions and an enchanting plot.

The structure of the book is divided into multiple parts, each consisting of several chapters that build upon Erin's experiences and the unfolding mystery surrounding her dreams. Williams skillfully crafts a narrative that oscillates between light and darkness, echoing Erin's internal battles with hope, fear, and the desire for connection. Themes of love, loss, and destiny resonate throughout, inviting readers to ponder their own relationships and the unresolved questions in their lives.

Williams' prose is lyrical and poignant, immersing readers in extraordinary settings—from marbled corridors to a vivid ocean lined with a sky-piercing tower. The author's ability to create a sense of urgency juxtaposed with ethereal beauty enhances the reading experience, making it both thrilling and deeply affecting.

While the book does delve into complex themes, it remains accessible and engaging for a wide audience. The inclusion of relatable characters, particularly Erin's dynamic with her adoptive mother, adds an extra layer of realism to the fantasy elements. *The Space Traveller's* Lover ultimately poses a fundamental question: What do we truly desire, and what lengths are we willing to go to attain it? Omara Williams invites readers to embark on this enchanting journey infused with hope, revealing the extraordinary within the ordinary.

A must-read for those who love their sci-fi infused with passion and high stakes.

# A Captivating Tale of Identity, Resilience, and the Struggle

Gwen McPhail's historical novel, My Place Among Them, masterfully intertwines personal history with compelling storytelling, exploring cultural identity, resilience, and the complexities of honouring the past while embracing the future.

# GWEN MCPHAIL

## BRINGS HISTORY TO LIFE WITH *"MY PLACE AMONG THEM"*

Editor's Desk I London

"A strong voice, first of all. The one thing that makes a novel unique is not so much the setting or the characters but the voice of the writer."

Gwen McPhail is not just an author – she is a storyteller with a rare capacity to weave history, family legacy, and cultural reverence into an exquisite narrative that resonates deeply with readers. Having spent over three decades imparting knowledge and nurturing young minds as a science and agriculture educator, Gwen's remarkable journey into literature is as inspiring as it is impactful. Her debut novel, *My Place Among Them,* written under the evocative pen name J. Stanion, is a masterclass in historical fiction that honours truth, tradition, and the intricacies of the human experience.

Drawing from an extraordinary manuscript passed down through her family, Gwen brings to life the stories of both John Iron Horse and Carter Heath– two compelling protagonists navigating the challenges of identity, heritage, and their inner moral compasses. Set against the backdrop of America's complex relationship with its Indigenous peoples at the turn of the 20th century, the novel reveals Gwen's unparalleled dedication to authenticity, achieved through meticulous research and collaborative consultation with the Lakota community. This is a book that not only transports its readers to another time but also offers a powerful lens through which to reflect on modern-day cultural and social dynamics.

Gwen's ability to infuse her characters with genuine emotion and depth is undoubtedly shaped by her years of teaching, where she observed the unfiltered joys, sorrows, and resilience of young people. Her commitment to preserving historical accuracy while delivering a compelling and compassionate story is further testament to her extraordinary skill as a writer. *My Place Among Them* is a novel rich with relevance, a labour of love that bridges generations and sheds light on stories both personal and collective.

In this exclusive interview, Gwen McPhail takes us behind the scenes of her debut work, sharing the inspirations drawn from her family's rich history and her intimate connection with the land and its stories. From the painstaking research process to her reflections on balancing historical fact with creative storytelling, Gwen's insights serve as a guiding light for aspiring authors and lovers of literature alike. Prepare to explore the heart and mind of a truly remarkable storyteller whose voice and vision have enshrined her place among contemporary literary greats.

### What inspired you to write "My Place Among Them," and how did your family's history influence the narrative?

"My Place Among Them" was taken from a manuscript written by my great-grandfather documenting his experiences with Indigenous people while working for the Bureau of Indian Affairs at the turn of the 20th century. For fear of losing his position, he never made his work public. It passed to his daughter and in turn to my father who died of cancer before he finished preparing the document for publication. He gave me the original document, along with his edited version, asking that I publish the story. I grew up listening to stories about both protagonists and hearing my father's respect for the Indigenous people of America both of which motivated me to see the work to completion.

### Could you elaborate on the research process you undertook to authentically depict the experiences of Indigenous peoples in your novel?

Inspired by family stories, I spent my childhood reading books about the Indigenous people of America. During my earliest edits of the manuscript, I reached out to living members of the Lakota tribe including elders on the Pine Ridge Reservation and archivists at Oglala Community College whenever details from the manuscript conflicted with what I thought I knew about Lakota culture. I had copies of letters and

McPhail's novel is a beautifully researched and deeply moving exploration of history, culture, and personal identity, capturing the essence of storytelling with authenticity and emotional depth.

employment records that referenced what my great-grandfather observed over his lifetime and internet access to rosters and administrative records of multiple schools run by the US Government from 1875 to 1955. I purchased a number of books recently written by Indigenous authors including an Indigenous history of America.

### How did your 31 years of teaching experience shape your approach to storytelling and character development?

Much of my teaching career was spent at the Middle School level, where I observed the emotional development of many children as they changed and matured over time. Every hurt, every joy, every nuance of emotion was on display almost every day in my classroom. I was involved with other teachers, administrators and parents, all of whom shared their personalities and emotions over the years. Teaching requires a certain amount of entertainment skill to keep students focused, and I honed those skills over my 31 years in the classroom. I believe my teaching experience allowed me to close my eyes and immerse myself in memories that gave life to my characters and details to their actions in various settings.

### In what ways do you hope readers will connect with the character of John Iron Horse and his journey?

I hope that readers will connect with John's habit of seeking out quiet moments to reflect on the events of his life and their impact on his future and to seek guidance from his cultural heritage. Likewise, I hope they will find value in Carter's persistence in striving to achieve his own personal definition of success amidst the demands of a bureaucracy where success was often defined only by power and money.

### Can you discuss the significance of the novel's title, "My Place Among Them," in relation to the themes explored?

"My Place Among Them" is the story of two men who struggle to succeed in the world they live in. John Iron Horse strives to find his place in a society that is foreign to his heritage while Carter endeavors to find happiness in a bureaucracy he frequently disagrees with. It is the story of their efforts to do what they believe is right without giving up their individual values and identity.

### How do you balance historical accuracy with creative storytelling in your writing?

For historical fiction, it is important to immerse the reader in a specific time and place in history. I use precise descriptions of places, events and emotions that impact my characters to help the reader engage with the story. Sometimes this results in long passages that can be boring without meticulous editing to keep the reader focused. However, I make every effort to avoid graphic depictions of violence or sex, preferring to leave those vignettes to the reader's imagination.

### What challenges did you face in bringing the historical context of the late 1800s to life for contemporary readers?

For me, the hardest part of writing this story for contemporary readers was editing the often stilted, Victorian-era wording of the original manuscript while honoring the propriety of the era. It was hard, personally, to change my great-grandfather's long sentences and often verbose exchanges between characters. Having reviewed the original work hundreds of times, it was difficult to portray complex emotions with more modern words, particularly because, at the time, emotions were often hidden behind strict cultural mores that contemporary readers might not appreciate. It was also difficult to portray the harshness of life on reservations without focusing solely on violence and poverty.

### As an author, what advice would you offer to those looking to write historical fiction that honours the cultures and histories it represents?

It is imperative that an author know the details and history of the culture they are writing about and understand that there are usually multiple "sides" to every historical event. In depth research is important because readers pick up on errors in historical content quickly and may question the authenticity of the story or, worst of

*My Place Among Them* by J. Stanion is a moving exploration of cultural identity, resilience, and the clash between oppression and understanding. Brilliantly crafted, its profound characterisation of John Iron Horse and Carter Heath is deeply affecting. This award-winning historical fiction captures a dark yet essential chapter of history with sensitivity and authenticity.

all, simply put the book down.

### What particular skills do you look for in a writer of historical fiction?

A strong voice, first of all. The one thing that makes a novel unique is not so much the setting or the characters so much as the voice of the writer. Too many historical novels feel the same — the setting has changed, but the book could have been written by anyone. So what really sets it apart, and the first thing I look for, is a strong author voice. That being said, a strong sense of history and adequate research so that the story feels genuine are essential, of course. I want a story that's unique and interesting, so it's best if the writer has a passion for that particular period or the events surrounding the novel. I suppose I also prefer an author with a good vocabulary, particularly appropriate to the setting and time. I like to see a clear sense of mood. Good rhythm to their words. Clear pacing. Great characters in interesting situations. Strong dialogue. Vibrant scenes. Action or events that move me from one page to the next. And, if it's to have a longlasting quality to it, themes that are greater than boy-meets-girl (which works fine in a historical romance, but we like to see more in a true historical saga).

# Memoir of Identity, Courage, and Cultural Discovery

Jobert E. Abueva reflects on his international upbringing, hidden identities, and writing process behind Boy Wander, offering heartfelt insights on resilience, vulnerability, and the liberating power of telling one's truth.

"Navigating those contrasting identities was like walking a tightrope between two distinct, yet equally vital worlds."

# JOBERT E. ABUEVA

## SHARES HIS GLOBAL COMING-OF-AGE JOURNEY IN BOY WANDER

as told to Dan Peters

Jobert E. Abueva stands as a luminous figure in contemporary literature, emerging as an award-winning author whose voice resonates with authenticity and profound insight. With his memoir, *Boy Wander – A Coming of Age Memoir,* Abueva invites readers into a rich tapestry of his experiences, spanning vibrant cities such as Manila, Kathmandu, Bangkok, and Tokyo. This captivating narrative not only recounts his personal journey but also reflects the unique cultural influences that shaped his identity and understanding of the world.

As the inaugural recipient of the Lambda Literary J. Michael Samuel Prize and winner of several prestigious literary contests, Abueva's accolades speak to the impact of his storytelling. His ability to weave intricate tales that explore themes of identity, acceptance, and resilience showcases a mastery that transcends mere memoir writing. The critical acclaim he has garnered, including recognitions from literary institutions and notable publications such as *The New York Times* and *The Philadelphia Inquirer*, further underscores his compelling contribution to the literary world.

Through our interview, Abueva's depth of insight into the dualities of life, particularly in navigating contrasting identities and challenging personal experiences, emerges as both thought-provoking and inspirational. His reflections on the era preceding the AIDS epidemic and its profound effect on his understanding of sexuality resonate powerfully, shedding light on a pivotal time in history. Moreover, his journey from the cultural revolutions of the 1960s and

70s to his arrival in America illustrates a universal quest for self-acceptance that many readers will find relatable.

*Boy Wander* is more than just a memoir; it is a testament to the transformative power of storytelling. Abueva's guidance for aspiring authors, particularly in embracing vulnerability and authenticity, serves as a beacon for those seeking to navigate their own narratives. As Reader's House magazine proudly showcases this interview, we celebrate Jobert E. Abueva not only as a remarkable author but also as a voice of inspiration, encouraging us all to embark on our journeys of self-discovery and connection.

**'Boy Wander' details your life across Manila, Kathmandu, Bangkok, and Tokyo. How did these diverse cultures influence your personal journey?**

Each of these cities from my boyhood left a unique imprint on who I am. In Manila, where I was born, I learned of resilience and warmth amid political upheaval and where community and family are deeply intertwined. Kathmandu introduced me to a world of spiritual depth; its majestic landscapes and mystical rituals nurtured a reflective and introspective side of me. The same goes for Bangkok which was a celebration of contrasts—the energetic vibrancy of street life, the fusion of old and new, and

> Abueva's voice is fearless, elegant, and profoundly human—his memoir illuminates the complexities of identity with striking honesty and emotional resonance.

a palpable pulse that taught me spontaneity and adaptability. Then there's where I spent my high school years, Tokyo, a city where precision meets tradition, inspiring discipline and an appreciation for the subtle beauty of everyday moments.

These diverse cultures wove into the fabric of my personal journey and to this day my career remains global in scope, and I am nomadic by nature. They have enriched my understanding of what it means to belong and helped me embrace the beautiful complexity of my own identity. The lessons I gleaned from each place have fueled my narrative, shaping Boy Wander into a memoir that is as much about finding home in the world as it is about finding oneself.

**Your memoir reveals a dual life as a high-achieving student and a clandestine existence at Tokyo's Imperial Hotel. How did you navigate these contrasting identities during your youth?**

Navigating those contrasting identities was like walking a tightrope between two distinct, yet equally vital worlds. On one side was the disciplined life of a high-achieving student—a realm where expectations were clear and every success, academic and otherwise, was measured against a strict internal bar set by family and society. On the other, there was the clandestine existence at Tokyo's Imperial Hotel, a place where the usual rules dissolved, allowing me to explore a deeper, perhaps wilder, and often misunderstood part of myself.

The key was compartmentalization to live in both realms without letting one overpower the other. I learned to switch gears, being adept at keeping things, er, straight. A more complex, resilient identity took shape, which is the narrative thrust behind Boy Wander. Ultimately the journey to self-understanding is rarely linear, and embracing our contradictions is what makes our stories rich and real.

**In 'Boy Wander', you discuss your experiences before the advent of AIDS. How did this era shape your understanding of sexuality and identity?**

Even as an adolescent, reading the initial headlines of a gay cancer, I sensed that my encounters, as thrilling and daring as they were, were also entering an unchartered, guarded zone that by the time I arrived in America, made me reconsider how promising this new land of opportunity may be.

I discovered that sexuality was not merely a series of physical encounters, but a profound window into who I was becoming. Our interactions, free from the pervasive fear that would later grip our community, allowed me to embrace a more spontaneous and, in many ways, innocent exploration of self. This era taught me that sexuality and identity are intricately entwined—each encounter, each secret meeting early on, was a step toward understanding the depth of our own humanity. The absence of AIDS did not mean there was no risk; it was an environment in which emotional and social risks were taken without the immediate weight of a looming epidemic. In retrospect, I realized that this unguarded exploration, while beautiful, also set the stage for a later reckoning, time when our freedoms were suddenly redefined by loss, fear, and the urgent need for compassion.

**Your story spans from the 1960s and 70s to your arrival in America. How did these different time periods affect your self-acceptance journey?**

The 1960s and 70s were marked by cultural revolution and personal experimentation as well as charged with the energy of rebellion and artistic exploration, when I was boldly testing the boundaries of who I was expected to be. I eventually learned that self-acceptance was not something handed down by society; it had to be forged through introspection, risk, and often a quiet defiance

*Boy Wander* is Jobert E. Abueva's candid coming-of-age memoir, chronicling his double life as a high-achieving student and secret sex worker in 1970s Tokyo. Spanning continents and decades, it explores identity, resilience, and acceptance, offering a poignant reflection on navigating societal expectations while staying true to oneself.

of conventional norms. However, this was also a time marked by internal conflict and isolation, as traditional (Catholic) values still loomed large and made it challenging to fully embrace every facet of my emerging identity.

Arriving in America introduced me to a whole new dynamic. The cultural landscape was both liberating and complex, and where I could explore my authentic self even further. Yet, this new freedom came with its own set of challenges—reconciling my global roots with the pressures to assimilate and find a balance between the daring independence of my past and the expectations of a new society.

### 'Boy Wander' has received multiple accolades, including the Book Excellence Award and Reader's View Bronze Award. How have these recognitions impacted you?

Receiving accolades like those mentioned and others since has been both humbling and rewarding. Such recognitions have affirmed that the deeply personal journey I shared in Boy Wander resonates with a diverse community of readers. They validate that being honest about my struggles and triumphs isn't just cathartic—it's a powerful connection point that others value. Moreover, they have fueled my creative spirit, to keep pushing with my writing. A nice biproduct is that awards open doors to connect with readers, fellow writers, and communities who see reflections of their own journeys in my work. This broader recognition not only spreads my story further but also fosters deeper discussions about identity, cultural crossovers, and the evolving nature of self-acceptance. And I do hope it inspires others to write with brutal honesty and vulnerability.

"Such recognitions have affirmed that the deeply personal journey I shared in Boy Wander resonates with a diverse community of readers... They validate that being honest about my struggles and triumphs isn't just cathartic—it's a powerful connection point that others value."

### Your writings have appeared in publications like The New York Times and The Philadelphia Inquirer. How has your journalistic work influenced your memoir writing?

My work as a freelance journalist has enriched my approach to memoir writing. In journalism, every word counts. Crafting articles that are both factual and engaging taught me to choose my words deliberately, an invaluable skill when recounting personal memories. This precision helped me present my experiences in Boy Wander with both clarity and depth. Journalistic writing demands a delicate balance between reporting facts and evoking emotion. This journey allowed me to navigate the personal terrain of my memoir with authenticity, ensuring that while the narrative remains raw and deeply personal, it also resonates with a broader audience through contextual accuracy and clarity. My narrative lives through the Vietnam War, martial law in the Philippines and the U.S. Bicentennial, among other world events.

My journalistic background has provided me with the tools to distill complex personal experiences into a narrative that is both rigorously edited and intimately affable. It's a continuous interplay between the meticulous care of fact-checking and the fearless exploration of memory, ensuring that every piece of my story carries the weight of truth as well as the raw beauty of being human.

### As a storyteller who has performed on stage, how does live storytelling compare to writing for you?

For me, live storytelling is like stepping into a shared heartbeat of the moment, while writing is a quiet conversation with my own inner truths. When I'm on stage, I feel a contagious energy, the audience's laughter, gasps, or even reflective silence feed into my delivery. The immediacy of live performance makes vulnerability palpable; I'm giving my story directly, and that raw connection, that spark of mutual understanding, is incredibly exhilarating. Writing, on the other hand, is a solitary, meticulous craft. It allows me to sift through memories, layer them with reflection, and polish each nuance at my own pace. It's like sculpting my past—revisiting each detail, reshaping it until it mirrors the truth I want to share. Both modes of storytelling reveal a slice of my truth with the intent of connecting with others.

### What advice would you offer aspiring authors, especially those writing about personal and challenging experiences?

The journey of writing, especially when it is about personal and challenging experiences, is both brave and transformative. Rember that every life is unique, and your story is yours alone. Embrace the raw authenticity of your experiences. Do not shrink from the parts that feel painful or messy; those are often the parts that hold the greatest truth and potential for healing—not just for you, but for your readers as well. It sure has been the case for me.

Delving into personal history can uncover old wounds. Give yourself permission to feel and, if necessary, take breaks. (It took me 20 years, on and off, to complete my memoir!). Remember that while your writing is a gift to the world, it's also a deeply personal process. Establish safe spaces in your routine where you can write without judgment or haste.

Also, connect with trusted peers, mentors, or writing groups who understand the delicate balance of vulnerability and craft. Their feedback can help you polish your work without diluting your authentic voice. Three distinct writing groups have reviewed chapters of Boy Wander. And I am grateful to every one of them.

Writing about personal challenges is both an act of courage and a gift to others. Your vulnerability has the power to connect, heal, and inspire, so trust your voice, be patient with your journey, and know that every step, however painful, is paving the way to a more authentic and compassionate existence.

# Kelly Elliot Dazzles Readers With Her Tender, Transformative Tales Of Romance And Life

by ELEANOR WILSON

## Romance Reimagined Through Courage And Life-Changing Writing

Kelly Elliot poses with a thoughtful smile, radiating her creative passion and the warmth of her enchanting small-town inspirations.

Kelly Elliot continues to enchant readers with her masterful blend of sweet romance and poignant exploration of life's most delicate issues. In our exclusive interview, she reveals the journey behind her dual identity—as both the beloved Kelly and the dynamic Ellie Grace—and offers insights into the creation of intricately detailed worlds that captivate the hearts of fans worldwide. A New York Times and USA Today bestselling author, Kelly's ability to interweave contemporary romance with themes of resilience, hope, and real-life challenges truly sets her apart. Her novels, whether they transport you to the comforting ambience of a small-town setting or take you on an emotional rollercoaster tackling subjects like miscarriage, PTSD, and infertility, are celebrated for their authenticity and deeply resonant narratives.

In our conversation, Kelly candidly discusses the pivotal moments that have defined her career and the art of balancing emotional storytelling with her own experiences. Her advice for budding authors—and a glimpse into her disciplined writing routine and the joy of playing with different genres—further highlight a remarkable journey from self-published beginnings to literary acclaim. Join us as we delve into the life of an author whose works not only entertain but also offer solace and inspiration to countless readers.

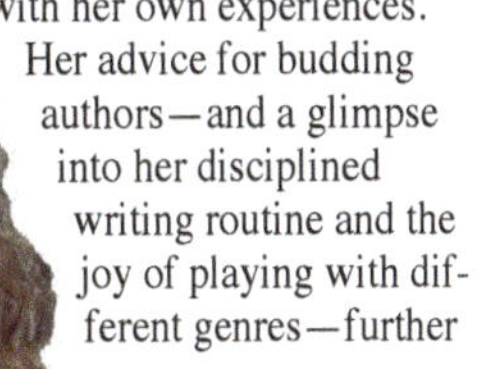

**Your journey as a self-published author to a USA Today and New York Times bestselling writer is truly inspiring. What was the turning point in your career that made you realise your books were resonating with readers on such a large scale?**

It was probably when I received emails after my second book, Saved, was published. It dealt with miscarriage and Fragile X. Women wrote to me and thanked me for talking about miscarriage and how it didn't make them feel so alone. A number of other people wrote to me about Fragile X syndrome. That was when I truly knew that even though I was telling a love story, I could still write about things that meant something to someone. I've since wrote about suicide, PTSD, endometriosis, and infertility, and wove those subjects around a love story.

**Your novels are known for their deep emotional connections and heartwarming romance. How do you craft such authentic and relatable love stories, and do you draw inspiration from real-life experiences?**

I love storytelling and I've always got ideas floating around in my head. I do draw from real-life experiences, yes and always try to include something personal from my life in ever single story I write.

**Many of your books, like the Wanted and Meet Me in Montana series, capture the charm of small-town settings. What draws you to write about these places, and how do you ensure each town feels unique and immersive for your readers?**

I live in a small town and my husband grew up in a small town. His family had a 500 acre ranch, so I spent a lot time there with him early on in our relationship. I love writing about a town where you can close your eyes and picture it. Each time I write a story, I want to create a world my readers can get lost in.

**As a prolific author, how do you balance your writing schedule with personal life, and what advice would you give to aspiring writers trying to maintain consistency in their craft?**

I try to write something, even its just a few hundred words each day. I also use Pacemaker which creates a schedule for me to follow and that helps to keep me on track. One thing I learned early on is that I needed to make time for my personal life. Being a writer can be very lonely so be sure to have a small group of people, whether they are writers or not, that you can talk to each day. And don't keep going back and reading what you write. Get it all down and once you're finished you go back and tweak it as you read it.

**You've written across multiple romance subgenres, from contemporary to western romance. Is there a story or genre you haven't explored yet but would love to write one day?**

Historical. I love reading historical romance. I dove into historical romance one time with a book I co-wrote and I adored it. Probably my favorite book I've written to date. It is no longer published, but I loved immersing myself into another time.

SOURCE: MOSAIC DIGEST

> *"I love storytelling and I've always got ideas floating around in my head. I do draw from real-life experiences, yes and always try to include something personal from my life in ever single story I write."*

**Kelly Elliott**
NEW YORK TIMES BESTSELLING AUTHOR

## Award-Winning Author Of The Crossover Series

Joseph Schwartz discusses his fantasy worlds inspired by the American West, his passion for storytelling, and the family ties that drive his characters.

# JOSEPH SCHWARTZ

## *THE STRESS DOC BRINGS WISDOM, HUMOUR, AND COMPASSION TO MENTAL HEALTH AND CHILDLIKE WONDER*

Editor's Desk I London

"I teach my students to write with power and precision. Do I practice what I teach? Read my stories and find out!"

Joseph Schwartz is a remarkable storyteller whose literary journey offers a vivid exploration of adventure, family, and the complexities of human relationships. Born in the serene landscapes of Havre, Montana, and later making his home in the bustling city of Phoenix, Arizona, Schwartz draws upon his rich upbringing to craft novels that resonate deeply with readers. His current project, the Thomas Berenford Chronicles, showcases his ability to blend fantasy with reality, weaving intricate tales that reflect his passion for the American West and the human experience.

Schwartz's works, including the acclaimed Crossover Series, invite us into a world where fantasy collides with the everyday, challenging our perceptions of identity and belonging. His novel "The Crossover Test," which recently garnered a silver medal at the Global Ebook Awards, exemplifies his unique narrative style and ability to create compelling characters navigating the unknown. With a background as an English teacher, Schwartz imparts power and precision in his writing, encouraging readers to embrace the thrill of adventure and the intricacies of family dynamics.

The Thomas Berenford Chronicles, comprising novellas such as "Wilder Fire," "Blood Daggers," and "The Broken Coil," further demonstrate his masterful storytelling. Schwartz's writing pays homage to classic genres while introducing fresh perspectives and themes that resonate with audiences today. Readers will undoubtedly find themselves captivated by Schwartz's imaginative worlds and the timeless struggles of his characters, making this interview a worthy feature in the upcoming issue of Reader's House magazine. Join us as we delve into the mind of a truly gifted author whose works inspire and challenge us in equal measure.

*Wilder Fire* is an enthralling start to the Thomas Berenford Chronicles, blending sharp wit with a thrilling fantasy adventure. Joseph Schwartz masterfully crafts a world where danger lurks around every corner, showcasing Berenford's unique abilities and complex moral dilemmas. A captivating read for fans of swords and sorcery.

**How did your upbringing in Montana and subsequent move to Phoenix influence the settings and themes of your novels, particularly "The Crossover Test"?**

The influences come from the American West, with all the mountains, lakes, rivers, fields, and roads provide the setting. More importantly, this majestic landscape calls upon the man and women courageous enough to answer the question; are you ready for adventure? Finally, the novel explores family relationships: the troubles, the bonds, the love.

**The Crossover Series explores the premise that this world is populated by secret crossovers from another dimension. How did that idea come to you?**

Stephen R. Donaldson writes several epic fantasy novels about a man transported to a realm called The Land. I flip that premise on its head; what if two talented brothers, James and Rory, both from a fantasy realm, were transported to this realm? How do they fit in? How do they survive the threat of a shapeshifting assassin? The result is the Crossover Test and the sequel, the Crossover Brand.

A confident, imaginative storyteller with a unique take on classic fantasy and thrilling supernatural elements.

**"The Crossover Test" won the silver medal at the Global Ebook Awards. How did this recognition impact your writing career and future projects?**

The recognition was like a cattle prod to my ego! With that surge, and some new confidence, I wrote the sequel, "The Crossover Brand".

**Can you discuss the development process of the sequel, "The Crossover Brand," and how it expands upon the original story?**

"The Crossover Brand" begins tree years later, with brothers Conrad separated. The story places the focus more on Rory, the talented but troubled younger brother with the power to rend apart the fabric of the universe. Two major characters are added, as well as more development for the Censorum, the chief protagonists and arbiters of hatred, judgement, and discord.

**As an English teacher since 1998, how has your teaching experience shaped your writing style and approach to storytelling?**

I teach my students to write with power and precision. Do I practice what I teach? Read my stories and find out!

**Your current project is the Thomas Berenford Chronicles. Who is this protagonist and what is that character all about?**

Thomas Berenford is the father of the two main characters in the Crossover Series, James and Rory, who are yet to be born. Berenford lives in the Outer Realm, a fantasy setting that mirrors this world: same mountains and valleys, same bodies of water. Legend has it that even the blades of grass are the same. Unlike here, magic and power rule. If you can swing a sword, you may prolong your demise. Thomas wants none of that hot mess, but of course, he will never escape it.

**The Thomas Berenford Chronicles currently include three novellas: "Wilder Fire", "Blood Daggers", and "The Broken Coil". What ideas, themes, and styles run through these stories?**

The series is a callback to classic swords and sorcery from authors Fritz Leiber and Robert E. Howard. For a template of motif and structure, I called upon film genres: detective noir, mob movies, and classic westerns.

# Celtic Mythology Meets Roman History

Linnea Tanner discusses interweaving Celtic mythology with Roman history, crafting complex characters, blending historical accuracy with fantasy, and her personal inspirations, including ancient warriors and her transformative travel experiences to archaeological sites.

# LINNEA TANNER

## *WEAVES MYTH AND HISTORY INTO TIMELESS TALES OF ANCIENT ROME AND BRITANNIA*

Editor's Desk I London

"The cultural conflict between the prosaic, realistic Romans and the mystical, nature-oriented Britannic tribes provides a major conflict in the series."

Linnea Tanner's literary mastery showcases a dazzling interplay of historical authenticity and mythical imagination, making her a standout voice in the realm of historical fiction enriched with Celtic mythology. A true luminary in her craft, Tanner doesn't merely write stories; she conjures immersive worlds brimming with political intrigue, forbidden love, fierce battles, and the enigmatic tension between Roman imperialism and Britannic mysticism. Her award-winning *Curse of Clansmen and Kings* series—a tapestry elegantly woven with titles like *Apollo's Raven*, *Dagger's Destiny*, *Amulet's Rapture*, and *Skull's Vengeance*—is a testament to her dedication to vivid storytelling and meticulous research. Additionally, her poignant short story, *Two Faces of Janus*, demonstrates her ability to delve deeply into the human condition within the historical context of Ancient Rome.

Inspired by the indomitable spirit of women like Boudicca, Linnea crafts heroines who defy adversity, and through their journeys, she explores universal themes of love, power, resilience, and identity. Her protagonist, Catrin, is a force to be reckoned with—a Celtic warrior princess with Druidic abilities whose evolution from innocence to sovereignty captures the hearts of readers. With an academic foundation in chemistry paired with an undying passion for history and mythology, Linnea seamlessly blends rigorous archaeological research with the imaginative flair of fantasy to bring the ancient world to life.

In this exclusive interview, Linnea Tanner takes us behind the scenes of her captivating narratives, reflecting on the inspirations, cultural clashes, and mythical underpinnings that shape her tales. Her travels to historical sites, her fascination with Arthurian legends and the legacy of Mark Antony and Cleopatra, as well as her dedication to interweaving history with fantasy, reveal the mind of an author deeply committed to her readers and her craft. It is with great admiration that we invite you to meet the brilliant mind behind stories that transport us to the mystical and tumultuous realms of Ancient Rome and Britannia.

**How has your background in chemistry influenced your approach to writing historical fiction, particularly in integrating detailed research into your narratives?**

My background in chemistry provides a basis on how I research historical books, academic papers, and archaeological findings to support my work. The Celts left almost no written records. Their historical events were supplanted by Greek and Roman historians, archaeological findings, and medieval writers who spun their Christian beliefs into the Celtic mythology they wrote about.

**Your 'Curse of Clansmen and Kings' series intertwines Celtic mythology with Roman history. What inspired you to blend these two distinct cultures in your storytelling?**

The series is inspired by Boudicca, a Celtic warrior queen and druidess who united the Britons in a rebellion against the Romans in AD 61. The Celts held women in higher esteem than the empire-building Romans. The cultural conflict between the prosaic, realistic Romans and the mystical, nature-oriented Britannic tribes provides a major conflict in the series.

**Catrin, the protagonist in your series, is a Celtic warrior princess with Druidic abilities. How did you develop her character, and what aspects of her journey do you believe resonate most with readers?**

Linnea Tanner captivates readers with her intricate storytelling, richly imagined worlds, and masterful blend of history, mythology, and fantasy.

The series is a coming-of-age story of Catrin who must transform from a naïve Celtic princess into a formidable warrior queen. She is tested in ordeals so she can gain newfound wisdom and power to overcome her treacherous half-brother, King Marrock. Modern-day audiences will relate to her emotions of love, grief, and heartbreak as she courageously faces what seems insurmountable circumstances.

**In 'Skull's Vengeance', Catrin faces her sorcerer half-brother, King Marrock. Can you share insights into crafting their complex sibling rivalry and its significance to the overarching plot?**

The sibling rivalry between Catrin and King Marrock drives the overarching plot. The first book in the series, Apollo's Raven, begins when Catrin's father reveals that she is the raven and Marrock is Blood Wolf in the curse cast by the previous queen, Marrock's mother: "I prophesy your future queen will begat a daughter who will rise as a raven and join your son, Blood Wolf, and overtake your kingdom." Catrin must break the curse by altering the future which may have unforeseeable consequences. Not only is the tale about her conflict with Marrock, but it is also about her internal struggle not to transform into someone as evil as him as she gains new magical powers.

**Your short story 'Two Faces of Janus' is set in Ancient Rome. How does this narrative connect to or diverge from the themes explored in your main series?**

One of the antagonists in the Curse of Clansmen and Kings series is Lucius Antonius, the father of Catrin's secret husband (Marcellus Antonius). Little is known about Lucius except he was the son of Iullus Antonius and grandson of Marcus Antonius (Mark Antony) and was banished to Gaul after his father's death. In Two Faces of Janus, Lucius must demonstrate his fealty to Augustus Caesar by witnessing the suicide of his father who is condemned to die for his treasonous adultery with the emperor's daughter. This tragic scene haunts Lucius throughout his life and impacts Marcellus's fate in the series.

**Having travelled to various archaeological sites for research, can you discuss a particular location that profoundly impacted your writing and how it influenced specific scenes or settings?**

An eleven-mile hike on the Dover Cliffs inspired the first scene of Catrin spotting warships that suddenly appearing out of the mist in Apollo's Raven. The Roman lighthouse at the Dover castle evoked the image of a fortress being built by King Marrock with the aid of Romans in Skull's Vengeance. The ruins of the Amphitheatre of the Three Gauls in Lyon, France elicited an image of Catrin parading up the steep road to combat as a female gladiator at the arena in Amulet's Rapture.

**The series draws inspiration from Arthurian legends and the legacy of Cleopatra and Mark Antony. How have these historical and mythical elements shaped the themes and character dynamics in your work?**

Although the series takes place almost 500 years earlier, the cultural clash between the Celts and Romans are pivotal to the storyline. Some of Merlin's magic such as shapeshifting, controlling nature, and appearing and disappearing in a magical fog are depicted in the books. Before the Roman occupation of Britain in 43 AD, Britain may have been a client state like Cleopatra's Egypt under Roman influence but ruled independently by local monarchs. The conflict of love and duty is a similar theme in the series as the legacy of Mark Antony and Cleopatra.

**What advice would you offer to aspiring authors aiming to blend historical accuracy with elements of fantasy in their storytelling?**

My advice is to research the period and ascertain whether the events in the story are

*Skull's Vengeance* by Linnea Tanner is a compelling blend of historical fiction and fantasy. With richly descriptive prose, it follows warrior queen Catrin's dangerous quest to defeat her sorcerer half-brother. Featuring complex alliances, emotional depth, and unique magical elements, it's a thrilling conclusion to the *Curse of Clansmen and Kings* series.

historically plausible. For example, the backdrop of my series is based on evidence that Romans profoundly influenced British politics prior to their occupation of Britannia in 43 AD. Further, they should weave in fantastical elements as though it is the reality experienced by the characters.

# A Vibrant Journey Into Stress, Grief, And Creativity

Award-winning author Mark Gorkin discusses his innovative approaches to stress management, grief, and resilience, blending psychotherapy with humour and storytelling to create heartfelt connections and inspire emotional growth across generations.

# MARK GORKIN

## *THE STRESS DOC BRINGS WISDOM, HUMOUR, AND COMPASSION TO MENTAL HEALTH AND CHILDLIKE WONDER*

Editor's Desk I London

"Stress is not all bad; acute stress can be energising, motivating timely self-examination."

Mark Gorkin, affectionately known as *"The Stress Doc"*™ , is a force of nature in the fields of psychotherapy, motivational speaking, and mental health literature. A true luminary with an unorthodox edge, Mark has captivated audiences across mediums—stage, page, and screen—melding deep psychological insight with his trademark humour. His works radiate an authenticity and inventiveness that resonate with readers at every turn. Whether you're diving into the practical wisdom of *Practice Safe Stress*, confronting the raw vulnerability of *Fierce Longing…Fiery Loss: Relearning to Let Go, Laugh & Love*, or embarking on the lively adventures of *Where Is Charlotte?*, Gorkin's writing is a masterclass in blending profound human experience with wit, empathy, and playfulness.

With a career spanning decades, Mark has a repertoire that seamlessly bridges the emotional rigour of psychotherapy with the creative vitality of an artist. His Shrink Rap™ Productions and self-appointed Psychohumorist™ title reflect both his willingness to take risks and his dedication to breaking down complex topics—stress, trauma, grief, and resilience—into accessible, engaging, and often hilarious narratives. Books like *The Four Faces of Anger* and *Preserving Human Touch in a High-Tech World* are vivid demonstrations of his gift for distilling intricacies of the human condition into actionable insights, always punctuated with a knowing wink and nod.

In this interview, Mark opens up about the deeply personal inspirations behind his books, his creative process, and his mission to empower others through humour, imagination, and heartfelt connection. A read through his works or a conversation with him is a journey—at once therapeutic and entertaining, introspective yet profoundly relatable. Without further ado, Reader's House proudly presents the captivating thoughts and candid reflections of the legendary Mark Gorkin. Prepare to laugh, learn, and perhaps even roar like a tiger!

**How does your background as a psychotherapist influence the themes and approaches in your book *"Practice Safe Stress: Healing & Laughing in the Face of Stress, Burnout & Depression"*?**

Practice Safe Stress draws on my years of experience as a clinician and trauma-organizational consultant, as well my own personal experience dealing with burnout and depression. The book outlines and explores many manifestations of past and present trauma and loss – from the loss of health to the loss of a love. And offers "Safe Stress" models and strategies.

Perhaps most important, is sharing my own angst-filled journey, for example, burning out as a doctoral student. I reflect on my Phoenix-like transformation: a year later, discovering my "Psychohumorist" voice as a radio and TV "Stress Doc ™." I even began pioneering the field of psychologically humorous rap music, calling it, naturally, Shrink Rap ™ Productions. Poking gentle fun at my own flaws and foibles, I hope to role model the wise words, of psychoanalyst, Dr. Ernst Kris: What was once feared and is now mastered is laughed at. And as the Stress Doc inverted, What was once feared and is now laughed at... is no longer a master!

### In *"Fierce Longing...Fiery Loss: Relearning to Let Go, Laugh & Love,"* you explore grief and loss. What inspired you to write this book?

The inspiration is simple: My ex-partner had a granddaughter that I was crazy about; and the feeling was mutual. In fact, Charlotte's love of playing Hide-and-Seek with me was the catalyst for another book. (See question below.) I knew Charlotte from the time of her birth till she was 3 and-a-half. Alas, when my ex ended our ten-year relationship (our basic makeups were too discordant), the family thought it best to terminate my relationship with Charlotte. Without a doubt, it was one of the most painful losses on my life's journey. I did a lot of grieving in support groups; wrote a lot of angry

> Mark Gorkin's brilliance lies in his ability to transform pain into healing, using insightful humour, honest narratives, and boundless creativity.

and poignant poetry. "Fierce Longing" became a pathway for finding some peace, and eventually morphed into a vessel for all kinds of loss-inspired poetic writings, Shrink Raps ™, and psychological essays.

### Your children's book, *"Where Is Charlotte? Or Where Is ______?,"* combines psychology with playful poetry. How do you balance these elements to engage young readers?

The synergy of psychology and playful poetry is achieved by having a diverse and relatable character engaged in a universal and familiar adventure – e.g., the game of Hide-and-Seek. A little hero gets extra bonus points if she's fun and feisty. Charlotte's refrain when you incorrectly guess her hiding place... ("Is she in a cave of pillows"): "No she's not!"

Heartfelt connection occurs: 1) when your narrative is sung to the tune of a classic children's song, like Frere Jacque, 2) there's a simple and playful rhyme scheme, and 3) when captivating with colorfully vibrant, every day and fanciful illustrations. For example, Charlotte boldly proclaiming, "Even though you're bigger, I'll ROAR like a tiger," paired with a picture of a powerful tiger in the jungle. (And of course, kids and adults are encouraged to ROAR along with Charlotte.)

Finally, *Where Is Charlotte?* is more than just a reading experience: Children are encouraged to share their authentic voice, to affirm a clear "No," to howl and growl, jump up and down, and give loving "bear hugs" ... while imaginatively discovering their own hiding places.

### As a *"Motivational Psychohumorist,"* how do you incorporate humor into your writing to address serious topics like stress and trauma?

For starters, I like playfully edgy titles e.g, Practice Safe Stress, or my self-described Psychohumorist ™ moniker. (Of course, I let my audience decide where the emphasis on that word should go).

And when you can tweak a big ego, people usually love it. For example, a ditty to the tune of the old classic, "Tea for Two," now renamed "Humili-Tea for Two: The Narcissist's Version":

You for me, and me for me

Oh how nurturing you will be

Forget "To be or not to be"

Just simply think of Me, Me, ME!

As the acclaimed writer and humorist, Mark Twain, observed, "Wit is the sudden marriage of ideas which before their union were not perceived to have any relation." Consider this ironic pairing of the classical and psycho-comical:

My title for a radio program on burnout: Breaking out of a hell of a shell... Or, don't feel too sorry for Humpty Dumpty... he needed to hit bottom!

### Your work emphasizes stress resilience and trauma recovery. How do you ensure your writing remains accessible and relatable to a broad audience?

One way of capturing attention and insuring accessibility is using concise and clear, colorful and descriptive language. For example, highlighting the powerful stress symptom – muscle tension – such as neck or back pain, or the jaw- or teeth-clenching TMJ. Then I nonchalantly note, "We know what TMJ really stands for... Too Many Jerks! The outpouring of laughter reveals how many can relate.

Another tool is a brief and dramatic vignette:

I recall leading a stress workshop for VA Hospital nurse supervisors sitting around a boardroom table. The tension and angst were palpable. Then they introduced themselves: "Walker, W-16, Thompson, W-18, Jones W-20, etc." My immediate response: "It sounds like you are reporting from your battle stations." The sighs and nodding heads let me know I was on target. But what really convinced me of their burnout edge... the nurses two favorite slogans: "Do you eight and hit the gate. Nine to five and stay alive." These ladies knew chronic stress!

### Given your extensive experience in stress management, what are the most common misconceptions people have about stress, and how do you address them in your books?

Stress is not all bad; acute stress can be energizing, motivating timely self-examination: what am I feeling about the other, about myself; am I self-sabotaging, what new decisions and actions do I need to consider, am I ready to humble myself and ask for support or help? Chronic stress or hypervigilance is the danger. Remember, burnout is less

> Mark Gorkin's *Practice Safe Stress* is an engaging blend of humour, insight, and practical advice for managing stress, burnout, and depression. With its witty essays and actionable strategies, the book offers a fresh perspective on challenging topics. While some sections feel a bit overwhelming, it's a useful, lighthearted resource overall.

a sign of failure and more that you gave yourself away!

A powerful model is my "Four Stages of Burnout": 1) Physical, Mental, and Emotional Exhaustion; 2) Shame and Doubt, 3) Cynicism and Callousness, 4) Failure, Helplessness and Crisis. One gentleman accused me "of looking in his window"; he clearly saw himself in these stages.

Another favorite stress resilience and cognitive agility model is my formula for Natural SPEED – Sleep, Priorities & Passion, Empathy, Exercise & Diet. Using pithy poetry, I provide tools and tactics for surviving and striving. For example,

"P" stands for "Priority"

You can't do it all every day.

Urgent means now but important can wait.

Do you know how to "N & N"? –

Just say "No and Negotiate!"

### What advice would you offer to aspiring authors aiming to write about mental health and resilience in a way that is both informative and engaging?

Read the previous six answers. Just kidding. Perhaps a quote from a Nobel-Prize winning biochemist, Albert Szent-Gyorgi: See what everyone else has seen and think what no one else has thought. Come up with your own "Shrink Rap" ™ variation. Consider my new communication tactics – the New KISS and Memorable MISS: Keep it Short and Smart (compelling); and Make It Sassy and Surprising (captivating)!

In summary, be observant and listen to your gut. Jot down bullet points about surprising situations – whether they startle or evoke a knowing smile. (Like taking notes to remember a dream.) Then engage in exaggerated or imaginative play, while highlighting some cultural truth, some human flaw or foible. You want to ultimately help people laugh at their own vulnerable parts to encourage self- (and other-) compassion; to better accept our imperfect humanity. As I like to say, you don't just want to encourage empathy; you need to do more than just walk in another's shoes: True empathy is when you feel their bunions! (Amen and Women, to that!)

# Breaking Free from Beliefs and Embracing Awareness

Peter Ralston discusses his journey through consciousness studies, martial arts mastery, and enlightenment experiences, sharing deep insights on effortless power, breaking free from conditioned beliefs, and the pursuit of true understanding in life.

# PETER RALSTON

## SHARES PROFOUND INSIGHTS ON CONSCIOUSNESS, MASTERY, AND THE ART OF EFFORTLESS POWER

"Real grace, sensitivity, awareness, intelligence, and a calm mind are far superior to brute strength."

Peter Ralston is a true pioneer in the realms of consciousness, martial arts, and personal transformation. With a lifetime dedicated to the pursuit of truth—both in the physical domain of effortless power and in the profound depths of self-awareness—Ralston has reshaped the way we approach mastery, be it in movement, thought, or existence itself.

A foundational figure in the consciousness movement that flourished in the late 1960s and 1970s, Ralston's work stands at the intersection of deep philosophical inquiry and practical, real-world effectiveness. His relentless pursuit of understanding has led to groundbreaking contributions, not only in the realm of personal growth but also in the creation of his own martial art—the Art of Effortless Power—a discipline that redefines the nature of combat, presence, and interaction. His victory in the 1978 full-contact World Championship martial arts tournament in the Republic of China marked a historic achievement, solidifying his place as a master of his craft.

Beyond his martial prowess, Ralston's contributions to consciousness studies are unparalleled. Through books such as *The Book of Not Knowing, Pursuing Consciousness, and Ending Unnecessary Suffering*, he invites readers to dismantle conditioned beliefs, embrace direct experience, and cultivate an unshakable awareness of self and reality. His teachings challenge us to move beyond superficial understanding and into the realm of authentic, transformative insight.

In this interview, Peter Ralston shares his profound per

Peter Ralston is a true pioneer in the realms of consciousness, martial arts, and personal transformation. With a lifetime dedicated to the pursuit of truth—both in the physical domain of effortless power and in the profound depths of self-awareness—Ralston has reshaped the way we approach mastery, be it in movement, thought, or existence itself.

A foundational figure in the consciousness movement that flourished in the late 1960s and 1970s, Ralston's work stands at the intersection of deep philosophical inquiry and practical, real-world effectiveness. His relentless pursuit of understanding has led to groundbreaking contributions, not only in the realm of personal growth but also in the creation of his own martial art—the Art of Effortless Power—a discipline that redefines the nature of combat, presence, and interaction. His victory in the 1978 full-contact World Championship martial arts tournament in the Republic of China marked a historic achievement, solidifying his place as a master of his craft.

Beyond his martial prowess, Ralston's contributions to consciousness studies are unparalleled. Through books such as *The Book of Not Knowing, Pursuing Consciousness, and Ending Unnecessary Suffering*, he invites readers to dismantle conditioned beliefs, embrace direct experience, and cultivate an unshakable awareness of self and reality. His teachings challenge us to move beyond superficial understanding and into the realm of authentic, transformative insight.

In this interview, Peter Ralston shares his profound perspectives on martial arts, enlightenment, and the nature of consciousness itself. His insights are not merely intellectual—they are lived, tested, and honed through decades of rigorous contemplation and practice. As you read, prepare to question your assumptions, confront your beliefs, and glimpse a new way of seeing the world.

Peter Ralston is a visionary teacher whose groundbreaking insights on consciousness and effortless power continue to inspire and transform countless lives worldwide.

### How did your early experiences in Asia shape your approach to martial arts and consciousness studies?

When I was a child I lived in Singapore, I was invited by a Scottish friend to study Judo. But as a child it was just a game to me. I didn't even think it was a martial art until I came back the US and other kids informed me of this relationship. Most of my studies in the fighting arts, however, I learned in the US. But back then only Asians were considered good at these arts, so one of my goals became proving that a non-Asian could become a master in them. Having been raised in Asia, although certainly not the main factor, this perspective motivated me to some degree.

I think simply being exposed to different cultures and thinking contributed to my consciousness studies. From this exposure, I more readily recognized that no culture or thinking is true, they are all inventions. Most people are caught inside of the accepted belief systems and assumptions shared by their culture and have a hard time seeing what's true outside of those assumptions. Being able to see these cultural worlds for what they are and as basically false, helped me to view things outside of and independent of those limitations. Therefore, I was able to go more deeply into investigations and contemplations than is the norm.

### Can you explain the core principles behind the Art of Effortless Power and how they differ from traditional martial arts techniques?

After decades of studying and mastering pretty much every martial art ever invented, I began to see the limitations and myopic views they all have. Each lives in its own belief system and fantasy world that determines the views of that art. None are not true or necessary. After my consciousness breakthroughs, I was empowered to break free of all traditions and instead started studying the reality of fighting from the ground up, investigating every component involved in that relationship—what is perception, force, balance, body-being, power, timing, strategy, awareness, intent, states of mind, and everything else. From this truly open and grounded study, a far more effective relationship to fighting emerged.

I also saw that each art limited itself to a narrow field of study, focusing only on one or two martial possibilities—such as striking, throwing, grappling, tossing, kicking, or joint techniques. I didn't understand this limitation. It seemed to me that fighting should be well rounded and open ended, so I included it all in my art. Many people mistakenly think that to be effective and realistic, one must be simplistic and mechanical or strong and athletic. These assumptions are also unnecessary and untrue. Real grace, sensitivity, awareness, intelligence, and a calm mind are far superior to brute strength. As I say, skill always beats brute strength.

Commensurate with my investigations, since some traditional arts promised a form of mysterious or "internal" power, and in my mind didn't actually deliver, I set out to discover a truly effortless power for myself. It proved a challenging pursuit but was extremely rewarding and interesting. From this study I learned about many other possibilities I would have never conceived without the demands made on me to master real effortlessness. The spirit and core principles of this Art are being effortless and effective, intelligent and sensitive, rather than basing the practice on either fantasy or brute action as is the case with the majority of martial arts.

### What was the most profound realisation you had during your Zen contemplation and enlightenment experiences?

There is no self, there is no reality.

You don't live inside your head,

and existence isn't what you think or can conceive.

### How do you define "true consciousness," and what are the biggest misconceptions people have about it?

Most people are caught up in fantasies. It is easier to adopt some hearsay or belief rather than do the actual work. "True" consciousness is a direct personal encounter with whatever is true, independent from anything you might want to be true, or any beliefs you have. Only a direct encounter can inform you of what's what in whatever matter you are investigating or contemplating.

### Your books discuss breaking free from conditioned beliefs—what are some practical steps people can take to achieve this?

Read my books, do my workshops.

### How does the pursuit of mastery in martial arts relate to mastery in other aspects of life, such as business or relationships?

The pursuit of mastery can apply to any field. Setting the bar at mastery demands you learn and change, often radically. It pushes you to go beyond your own thinking and the thinking of any culture, and the unrecognized assumptions of humanity itself. It also forces you to delve into areas of experience and subjects you never would have thought to investigate otherwise. Once you grasp a principle in one domain, it is often applicable (in a different form) to others as well—that is if you truly understand the principle. Learning how to learn, understanding discipline and action, successfully relating to failure and correction, are all aspects of the pursuit of mastery, and will contribute to success in whatever you take on.

### What advice would you give to other authors looking to write about consciousness, mastery, or personal transformation?

Master what you want to write about first. Don't rely on the hearsay or the assumptions that accompany any endeavor. Find out and deeply experience for yourself what is really true, and then find a way to contribute it to others. Or, you could get a real job. :)

Peter Ralston's *Ending Unnecessary Suffering* explores how we create our own distress and offers contemplative practices to break free from it. By understanding mental patterns that cause suffering, we can cultivate awareness, control our thoughts, and achieve a more peaceful, complete life. This book provides a practical roadmap to inner freedom.

# Transforming Challenges into Aha! Moments

Ruth Fein discusses her inspiring journey with chronic cancer, blending journalism and advocacy, her book The Big C², and her mission to empower patients through storytelling and education.

# RUTH FEIN

## *REFLECTS ON TURNING LIFE WITH CHRONIC CANCER INTO INSPIRING STORIES AND PATIENT ADVOCACY*

Editor's Desk I London

"Each story is intended to leave the reader with an aha! moment."

Ruth Fein's remarkable literary journey is one of resilience, empathy, and purpose, and it is with great pleasure that we spotlight her in this issue of Reader's House. With a distinguished 40-year career gracing the pages of esteemed publications like The New York Times and a globe-spanning dedication to patient advocacy, Ruth stands as a luminary in health and life science writing. For more than three decades, she has lived with a rare chronic blood cancer—a deeply personal experience that has shaped her advocacy and writing, empowering countless individuals facing similar challenges.

Her profoundly moving book, *The Big C² – Stories from the Chronic Side of Cancer*, is a masterful tapestry of personal narratives and interviews with patients, caregivers, and renowned specialists. It not only offers vivid insights into the realities of chronic cancer but also inspires readers through moments of wit, wisdom, and poignancy. In this interview, Ruth shares her motivations, her unique methodology of blending journalism with advocacy, and her mission to demystify complex medical topics for diverse audiences. Her work resonates deeply, offering not only information but also hope and validation to cancer "thrivers" and their loved ones. It is an absolute privilege to share her wisdom and the incredible impact of her writing with you in this edition.

**In your book "The Big C² - stories from the chronic side of cancer," you weave together your own story with the experiences and insights of others. Could you discuss how your life with a chronic cancer shaped the narratives within the book?**

I don't know anyone who hasn't been personally touched by cancer. Living with a rare, invisible blood cancer for 30 years fills my head and heart with experiences others could benefit from reading – people living with cancer, their family and friends, their medical teams. I combined my own essays and life stories with interviews I conducted with people affected by cancer, including prominent specialists, even an end-of-life doula who speaks to what everyone over the age of 18 ought to think about and plan.

As a reader, I am most rewarded when I want to reread a sentence just to enjoy the rhythm of the rhetoric or a perfectly poignant description. That's my goal in my writing, to create an enjoyable read, even when the subject is as serious as cancer.

Each chapter reflects a theme I have lived. For example, I often hear "but you look fine." While well-intentioned, it can feel like your symptoms and disease are discounted. I remember feeling like a cancer "imposter" with my waist-long curls next to dozens of patients donning headwraps and wigs in a leukemia waiting room. I centered an interview on this common experience so it is a part of someone else's story, in this case, Michele.

Though chemotherapy, exhaustion and missed social gatherings were a part of her regular routine for years, two of Michele's closest friends recently made comments that had her trying desperately to keep her raised eyebrows from freezing in place. "You are lucky you have never really felt bad," is the paraphrase she describes. "These were days that I didn't even want to get dressed . . . or get out of bed," she recalls thinking. Then she was hit by the common denominator. She never explained, even to her besties, how bad she was feeling.

Ruth Fein's powerful storytelling and tireless advocacy exemplify compassion, resilience, and the ability to inspire and empower others.

### What other themes do you address through the stories in your book?

There is no right or wrong way to live with cancer, or to support someone you love with cancer, or for that matter any chronic illness. Each story is intended to leave the reader with an aha! moment. Inspiration is between every line, sometimes with a chuckle and a tear on the same page. Advocating for yourself can be life changing (even life saving); dealing with the uncertainty of a chronic cancer; creating a mission-driven life alongside a cancer journey; the underrecognized physical and emotional effects of a cancer treated or cured years earlier. Scientific advances mean more people are living with cancer. Changing how we talk to and about these cancer "thrivers" is an omnipresent thread.

### How has your 40-year career as a health and life science writer influenced your approach to patient advocacy, particularly for rare blood cancers?

I think like a patient. I question like a journalist. I write to educate, empower and enlighten. My work as a freelance writer crossed over to patient advocacy when I first wrote about myeloproliferative neoplasms (MPNs) and my personal story in a piece for The New York Times in the middle of a raging pandemic. Hundreds of patients, family members and even practitioners thanked me. They were grateful to finally have an understandable piece they could share which explained the rare cancer they awoke to every day. This is when I realized the gap in knowledge, understanding and resources. So, I began to report for media outlets with broad cancer audiences. Others labeled me an advocate, as I was a patient-centered informant. When I cover a story or write a patient or researcher profile, I approach it with the skill of an interviewer and the inquiring voice of a patient.

### As a patient representative on the National Comprehensive Cancer Network's clinical guidelines panel, what key changes have you advocated for to improve patient care?

It is humbling to be the only patient member of an esteemed panel of 32 physician/scientist experts. I am happy to leave as a legacy one addition to the recommendations for physicians treating MPN patients. that can affect quality of life. It is now prominently recommended that physicians recognize this, regularly evaluate MPN patients for emotional/mental health, and offer support services as needed.

### Through the global webinars and podcasts you have hosted, including "The Other Side of Cancer," you engage with a wide audience. How do you address topics and ensure that speakers' content remains relevant and supportive for cancer patients and their families?

I am involved in multiple patient groups so I hear what is on their minds, what they want to know more about, where the gaps are in information. When I ask questions of experts, I am not hesitant to push for simpler explanations. I often ask them to explain things as if they were speaking to a school class of 11 and 12-year-olds.

### With your extensive background in ghostwriting, including medical textbook chapters, how do you balance maintaining the original voice of the author while ensuring the content is accessible to a broader audience?

Ghostwriting can take many forms. My formula is to interview the expert whose story or expertise I'm sharing, with additional research as needed. In one case, I travelled five hours every other week for six months to meet with the author. I then wrote a book of his stories, in his voice, with my improvements to improve interest, organization and quality.

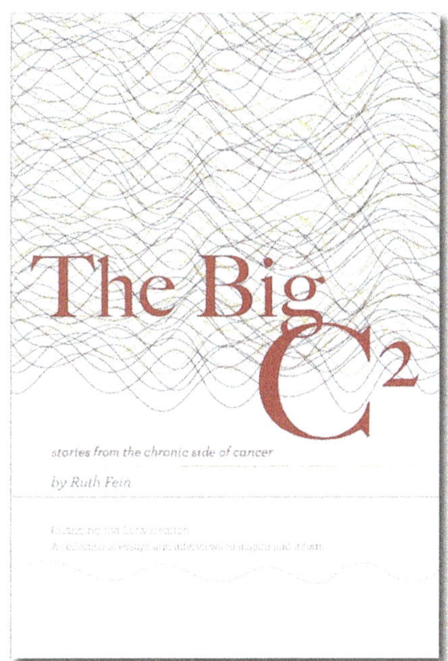


Ruth Fein's *The Big C²* is a compassionate and insightful exploration of life with chronic cancer. Blending personal experiences, interviews, and expert perspectives, it sheds light on navigating this complex journey. With its hopeful and empowering tone, it's an invaluable resource for patients, carers, and healthcare professionals seeking understanding and connection.

### Considering your experience in both writing and patient advocacy, what do you believe are the most effective strategies for conveying complex medical information to the general public?

Ask questions patients want answered. Q&As are a helpful, relatable format. If the reader can't explain what they have read to a 12-year-old, it is too complex.

### What advice would you offer to aspiring authors who wish to combine their personal health experiences with professional writing to advocate for others?

Consider what you want the reader to take away. Then, what format will work best to serve that purpose. Is it a memoir meant to inform or inspire others? Is it your own story combined with others' voices or expertise? Is a "how to" or academic approach best or creative non-fiction? Make an outline of your themes and take-aways. Speak to people in your intended audience and ask them what might make the book most meaningful.

# Crafting Complex Mysteries

Shaun Goldsmith discusses his inspirations, the intricacies of plotting The Spire, balancing mystery and thriller elements, crafting compelling characters, transitioning to screenwriting, and offering invaluable advice for aspiring writers.

Photo by David Chang

"Knowing the rules allows you to break them."

# SHAUN GOLDSMITH

## UNVEILS THE SECRETS BEHIND HIS AWARD-WINNING THRILLER THE SPIRE

Editor's Desk I London

Shaun Goldsmith is a name that has swiftly become synonymous with gripping detective fiction and masterful espionage thrillers. An award-winning author, Goldsmith has captivated readers with *The Spire*, a novel that seamlessly blends mystery, suspense, and intricate storytelling. Praised by *Kirkus* as "a fine whodunit full of satisfying twists," his work demonstrates a rare ability to craft narratives that are as intellectually stimulating as they are thrilling. His meticulous attention to detail, combined with a penchant for weaving together intricate plots, has earned him widespread acclaim and a dedicated readership.

With influences ranging from Ian Fleming and Agatha Christie to Robert Harris, Goldsmith has carved out a space where classic detective storytelling meets modern-day intrigue. His background—one that includes military service with top secret clearance and years spent teaching ESL in the Middle East—lends a unique authenticity to his work. These experiences have not only shaped his perspective but also enriched the depth and realism of his characters and plots.

Beyond the written word, Goldsmith's creative pursuits extend into the realm of film, with his thriller screenplay *Cold Autumn* currently in development. His ability to transition between mediums—capturing the essence of a story in both novel and screenplay form—speaks to his versatility as a storyteller.

In this exclusive interview with Reader's House, Goldsmith shares insights into his creative process, the inspirations behind his work, and the meticulous craft of constructing a compelling mystery. Whether you are a devoted fan or a newcomer to his work, his words are sure to offer a fascinating glimpse into the mind of one of today's most exciting crime and thriller writers.

**What inspired you to write The Spire, and how did you develop its intricate plot?**

The idea stems from the classic Agatha Christie mystery, "And Then There Were None." The key difference being the setting – not an island but a luxury skyscraper with a group of strangers being murdered one by one. Essentially, I was trying to create a locked room mystery inside a high-rise penthouse.

That said, I didn't want to create a traditional whodunit or police procedural. Instead, I decided to write a howcatchem'. This type of story requires intricate plot development. I used a variety of techniques – index cards, step outlines, reverse plotting. Ultimately, it comes down to time and research.

Above all, I wanted a story grounded in reality, and a page turner while being poignant and reflecting our times. I was gunning for gritty realism. I wanted to inject the story with the paranoia of "All the President's Men" and the true-life drama of "In Cold Blood."

> Shaun Goldsmith masterfully blends suspense, depth, and realism, crafting intelligent thrillers that captivate readers with intricate plots and unforgettable characters.

**Your book blends mystery, thriller, and police procedural elements—how do you balance these genres while maintaining suspense?**

Clearly understanding the rules, conventions and tropes of each. That allows you to apply them more freely and organically. Basically, I'm saying knowing the rules allows you to break them.

As well, pacing is key when it comes to suspense and technique is a major factor in that. One example is referred to as the Fleming sweep. The creator of James Bond, would 'sweep' the reader from one chapter to the next by means of a cliffhanger, adding tension and forcing them to turn the page. It's highly effective.

Nevertheless, with mysteries you cannot cheat! The author must give the reader the chance to solve the crime, which only adds to their suspense and engagement.

**'Diamond' Mike Vogel is a compelling protagonist—was he inspired by any real-life detectives or literary figures?**

Yes, and yes.

Like any of my characters, he is a combination of parts. Different pieces of a fictional human puzzle. Elements of him are inspired by both literary characters and real-life detectives. What was crucial as a protagonist was not to be the stereotypical American detective. Also, I did not want an all-knowing Sherlock Holmes/Hercule Poirot type. I wanted a genuine human being and authentic detective.

**Your bio mentions a military background with top secret clearance—did any of your experiences influence the storyline or themes in The Spire?**

Perhaps in some way. I think my military service was a desire for adventure and intrigue. However, most of my stories are built from research. It provides the avenues for your characters to go down.

Ultimately, my writing is a form of wish fulfillment. I'm just a middle-aged man who uses toy guns and cars to flesh out scenes and live vicariously through his work.

**How did your time teaching ESL in the Middle East shape your perspective as a writer?**

My teaching forced me to look at my own writing with a more critical eye. Although I find it tedious, revising your work is an essential step in the writing process. My time there made me a better editor of their work, and ultimately my own. Plus, it was the most rewarding job I've ever had.

**Your thriller screenplay Cold Autumn is in development—how does writing for film compare to writing a novel?**

Historically, there has been an argument as to which is harder. Frankly, I've never understood it. To me, it's as if two painters arguing which is better – watercolour or oil? Each has a distinct purpose. A screenplay is a blueprint. You are bound to put on the page only what you see and what you hear. Nothing else! You must write concisely with great brevity. In contrast, a novel allows you greater freedom to explore deeper, into the inner thoughts and feelings of a character.

Either way, they both must move with rhythm and flow. Otherwise, you bore the reader and that – whether you write scripts or novels – is the cardinal sin of writing.

**What advice would you give to aspiring authors looking to write complex and compelling stories like yours?**

Invest in the front end. Don't race to the keyboard. Plan your story. Know your story cold before you draft it. Follow the great Dame Agatha. Start with the murder. Build everything from there. Your villain creates the catalyst of your story. Who are they? What do they want? Why do they want it?

And of course, keep at it. Don't quit. Don't worry about writing a masterpiece. You must finish what you start.

Most of all, enjoy it! Love the writing you do. In the end, whatever fiction we write, we're all writing some sort of fairytale.

> Shaun Goldsmith's *The Spire* is a gripping, fast-paced thriller blending an intricate murder mystery with dark political intrigue. Detective Mike Vogel is a compelling lead, grappling with professional and personal challenges. Sharp prose, intricate twists, and chilling stakes make this a must-read for fans of crime fiction. Highly recommended.

# Unveiling Insights with

# SHERRY ARGOV

## Decoding Relationships, Empowering Women, and Redefining Love

EDITOR'S DESK | LONDON

Sherry Argov, the acclaimed author of Why Men Marry Bitches and Why Men Love Bitches, has captivated readers worldwide with her insightful take on relationships. Renowned as "America's Top Relationship Guide" by Book Tribe and hailed as one of the "Ten Most Iconic Books of the Past Decade" by Yahoo, Argov's influence extends far beyond the pages of her bestselling books.

With over 100 magazine features and appearances on national television shows like The Today Show and The View, Sherry Argov has become a household name in the realm of romance and self-empowerment. Her message resonates deeply with readers, challenging common misconceptions about love and urging women to embrace their independence and self-worth.

In this exclusive interview with Entrepreneur Prime Magazine, Sherry Argov delves into the inspiration behind her books, sharing insights gained from interviews with hundreds of men and offering practical advice for navigating the complexities of modern relationships. From debunking myths about romance to empowering women to stand up for themselves, Argov's wisdom shines through as she encourages readers to prioritize their own happiness and fulfilment.

As her bestselling books continue to soar to the top of international bestseller lists and inspire readers of all ages and backgrounds, Sherry Argov's universal message of self-confidence and empowerment transcends cultural boundaries. With each page turn, readers discover the transformative power of embracing their true selves and asserting their worth in every aspect of life.

Join us as we delve into the mind of this influential author and relationship expert, and uncover the keys to building healthier, more fulfilling partnerships in a world where love and self-respect reign supreme.

**Your books, *Why Men Love Bitches* and *Why Men Marry Bitches,* have been acclaimed as insightful relationship guides garnering significant attention and praise. What inspired you to write these books, and what do you hope readers will take away from them?**

Thank you for your kind words, which are very gracious. My inspiration came from the insightful feedback that I received from many men I interviewed who shared what they secretly respect and desire in a woman. It was very surprising to me to learn that the traits men want are the opposite of what most women believe. Most women believe they will be valued more if they try harder and do more to please their boyfriends or husbands. In my interviews with men, they explained that they do not want a woman who consistently sacrifices herself and who puts him on a pedestal. Instead, men desire and respect a woman who is more self-assured, independent and confident in herself, and less needy of reassurance from him. The message of my books is to always keep your life, maintain your independence and to pursue other interests outside of your relationship. My message to women is to always stand on your own two feet. Your happiness should not depend on another person.

OVER 1 MILLION COPIES SOLD!

WHY MEN LOVE Bitches®

From Doormat to Dreamgirl—A Woman's Guide to Holding Her Own in a Relationship

INCLUDES NEW CHAPTER!

—NEW YORK TIMES BESTSELLING AUTHOR—

SHERRY ARGOV

> Why Men Love Bitches by Sherry Argov explores why men are drawn to strong, self-assured women. Packed with witty insights and practical advice, it empowers women to command respect while maintaining romantic allure.

**Both of your books delve into the dynamics of romantic relationships and offer practical advice for women seeking to assert themselves and navigate the dating world more confidently. What are some common misconceptions about relationships that you address through your writing?**

Let's start with the misconception that if you are all-giving, overly generous and always available, you will get the same in return. Most women have given too much of themselves in a relationship and relate to the feeling of being taken for granted. My books explain why giving too much to someone (especially someone you've just met) may backfire, and why it doesn't always lead to the desired response from your partner in return. Successful relationships take time and people tend to value what they've earned. My books give specific examples that lead to a more balanced and successful relationship.

Another misconception is that a woman's beauty will lead to success in relationships. Most women are led to believe that if she is beautiful, a man will appear on a white horse, pay all her bills and solve all her problems. Yet beautiful women can have terrible relationships, while ordinary women are treated like queens. The men I interviewed desire a woman who has her own values, principles, goals, and a strong sense of who she is. They also shared that it's rare to find a woman who believes in herself. This is not just my opinion. It's what men told me over and over. A confident woman is never ordinary.

**In Why Men Love Bitches, and Why Men Marry Bitches you emphasize the importance of women standing up for themselves and maintaining their independence in relationships. Can you elaborate on why you believe these qualities are attractive to men, and how**

"Sherry Argov's profound insights and empowering message redefine love, inspiring women worldwide to embrace confidence, independence, and self-worth."

Why Men Marry Bitches: THE EXPANDED NEW EDITION is a game-changer! With humour and sisterly advice, Argov decodes the mysteries of relationships, empowering readers to embrace confidence and win the love they deserve. A must-read!

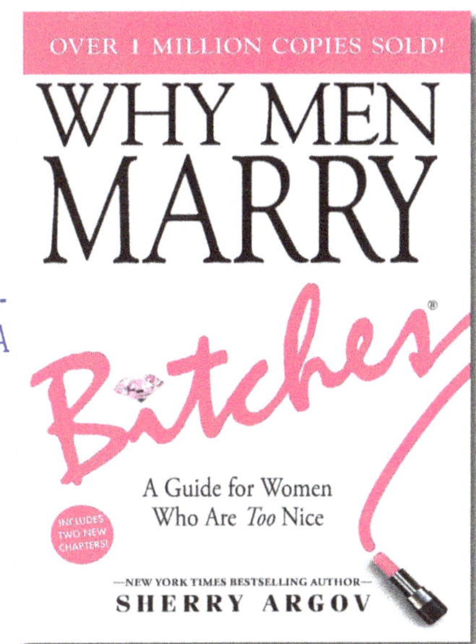


**they contribute to healthier and more fulfilling partnerships?**

Men like a challenge, and they want an equal partner. When a woman has a dynamic, interesting life, men want to be a part of it. It draws them in. Most men will be more appreciative that a woman who has to make time for him and they tend to work harder to become a part of that woman's life. When I talk about being a "challenge" I'm not only referring to how quickly a relationship is consummated in the bedroom. A woman who is a "challenge" doesn't move a man to the top of her priority list within the first week and pick up the phone on the first ring. She doesn't text multiple times a day. If she is interested in her own life, it shows. When a woman has goals, activities, interests and a fuller life outside of a relationship, and she isn't available all the time, most men will respect her time and attention much more.

**Your work has been featured in numerous magazines worldwide and you have made appearances on national television. How do you feel about the widespread impact and recognition of your books, particularly in influencing discussions about relationships?**

It is fulfilling to know that I have helped women and that I can earn a living doing something I enjoy. With regard to public recognition, it's a two-edged sword. Being in the public eye exposes you to people voicing their opinions online anonymously, and you don't always see the best side of human nature on the internet when they can hide behind a fake name. However, every day I am inspired by the many women who were helped by my books, and who feel much more confident and empowered after reading them. I enjoy hearing all the success stories from my readers.

**Your books have been translated into over thirty languages and continue to be bestsellers worldwide. What do you think contributes to the universal appeal and relevance of your insights on relationships across different cultures and societies?**

People from different countries may speak different languages, and eat different foods. But all human beings want love, dignity and respect. The emails that I receive from a woman in Europe will usually express the same feelings, insecurities, concerns and hopes as an email that I receive from a woman in India, or Latin America. Thank goodness for Google translate. The people who read my books are also very diverse in age. My audience includes men and women including pre-teens, college aged-women, middle-aged people, mothers, fathers, and senior citizens who are re-entering the dating scene late in life. I find it fascinating to see how similar we all are particularly in romantic relationships. If you're a woman reading this and you are struggling with something, you are not alone.

**As a bestselling author and relationship expert, what advice would you give to women who may be struggling to find their voice or assert themselves in their relationships? Are there any key principles or strategies from your books that you believe are particularly important for women to embrace in their romantic lives?**

When you begin to assert yourself, be clear, be respectful and speak your mind. Say what you mean and mean what you say. But don't say it meanly. It's never mean to let a man hear you speak your truth and see you stand up for yourself. When you believe in yourself, your partner will believe in you more as well. He will respect you more when you show respect for yourself. It's important to remember that a man should never be the reason you are happy. He should add to your happiness. Remind yourself daily that you are worthy and you deserve to be happy. It's a mindset. Choose your dignity and peace of mind over impressing others. Once you start to believe in yourself, things start to change for the better. Confidence is a superpower.

The inspiration behind The JJ Club are my two energetic boys—Jake and Joshua."

# Redefining Family Life with The JJ Club

Paul Kerslake shares how N3xus Global reintegrates ex-offenders into society through innovative technologies, strategic partnerships, and sustainable programs, creating lasting social impact while addressing workforce challenges across the UK, US, and EU.

# MOLLY HOOPER ALDRIDGE

## MOLLY'S SOLUTION FOR BALANCING WORK, HOME, AND FAMILY LIFE

as told to AJ SOMER | LONDON

Molly Hooper Aldridge is a trailblazing entrepreneur whose career has been defined by innovation, leadership, and a deep understanding of community needs. As the founder of The JJ Club, a luxury private members' club designed to support modern families, Molly has created a transformative space that caters to the unique challenges of balancing work and family life. With a vision that spans from tots to teens, The JJ Club is more than just a family hub—it's a lifeline for SW London families navigating the complexities of modern living. Molly's ability to blend her professional expertise with her personal experiences as a mother has resulted in a groundbreaking concept that is reshaping family life in her community.

Molly's entrepreneurial journey is nothing short of inspiring. From her early days leading global PR agencies to founding and scaling successful businesses, she has consistently demonstrated a knack for identifying gaps in the market and delivering innovative solutions. The JJ Club is no exception. Named after her two sons, Jake and Joshua, the club reflects Molly's passion for creating a space where families can thrive. With a robust digital platform, a curated events calendar, and partnerships with over 120 luxury brands, The JJ Club has already become a cornerstone for SW London families. As Molly prepares to open the club's first flagship site, her vision of a luxurious, family-focused space that combines work, play, and relaxation is set to redefine what it means to be a modern family in London.

> "I decided to solve the problem myself by creating a space that caters to all ages, not just kids."
> – Molly Hooper Aldridge

### What inspired you to create The JJ Club, and how does it reflect your personal experiences as a mother in SW London?

The inspiration behind The JJ Club are my two energetic boys - Jake & Joshua. I have been a busy working mum all their lives and as a family, we have always needed ongoing support to help with the modern juggle of work and family life - so fully understand the problem we're solving! There are not enough spaces locally catering for all our family needs and so I decided to solve the problem myself!

There are some amazing family clubs and communities across London and the wider country, but The JJ Club will be the first of its kind to really cater to all ages, rather than just babies and kids.

> Molly Hooper Aldridge is a visionary leader whose creativity, resilience, and passion are transforming family life and community connections.

### How do you envision The JJ Club evolving in the future to continue supporting families as they navigate the challenges of modern life?

Starting life as a digital club, The JJ Club will continue to add relevant brand partners and events to their online platform ensuring SW London families are benefiting from significant discounts across likeminded brands they know and love. In addition, more recommended professionals are often added into our Little Black Book of trusted experts (from dog walkers to interior designers to baby sitters), ultimately evolving us into a cornerstone for our SW London community with the opening of our first flagship club targeted to open late 2025.

### Can you share some of the key challenges you faced while transitioning from leading global PR agencies to founding a family-focused private members' club?

Assembling the right Avengers was critical: a team that is as passionate about building something special for families and has that depth & breadth in hospitality, operations and club membership. Learning to be entirely independent and wear every single hat requires resilience, passion and commitment - securing an advisory board and trusted local support has made a real difference here. I have found that some skills are very much transferable in terms of building out a business that people want to be a part of, creating a brand and club that members want to join, and leading a small but perfectly formed team of people. I'm used to the entrepreneurial rollercoaster and whilst this business is certainly my most personal and most ambitious yet I have learnt enough over the years to always ask for help, lean in to solving the little problems that crop up every day and drive on to deliver!

### How do your experiences in marketing and PR influence the way you approach brand strategy and community engagement for The JJ Club?

Having over twenty years' experience in PR & Comms has very much helped me in driving awareness, engagement and conversion of our digital club and brand. Having a clear business vision & values from the start alongside a consistent brand language and look & feel has allowed us to build out an engaged local community at pace. Ensuring all our brand messages are relevant to our community is key - and using organic social media channels, PR & Influencer engagement, and email marketing allows us to spread the word amongst this community, as well as word of mouth across our target market (particularly amongst the mums at the school gate.

### Can you elaborate on the types of events and experiences that members can expect from The JJ Club's curated events calendar?

We have a varied events calendar with 20+ events every month for our members, including Reformer Pilates, Kids' Cooking Class with Soft Play, Run Club, Cocktail masterclasses and more. While some of these events are included in our digital membership (£15 per month, £160 annual), others are ticketed separately, at a reduced members' rate. And many of our events are exclusive to The JJ Club so a great way to meet fellow members and locals. For non-locals we also run regular online events including sleep training workshops for little ones and tutoring workshops for 10+,11+ and 13+.

### How does The JJ Club's partnership with Little Village align with your vision of making a meaningful difference in the local community?

Our ethos is to make family life easier and make a positive difference in the community, and this includes supporting local charities who do so much for those in need. We launched with our charity partner Little Village who run a network of baby banks passing on loved goods from one family to another so that many more babies and young children have what they need to thrive. They also connect families into a wider network of support, helping them to build and extend their own 'village'. Little Village very much aligns with our own core business values of Passion, Playfulness, Courage, Kindness and Excellence so collaborating with them from the start and giving back to the local community was super important.

### What are some of the most popular perks and benefits that members have access to through The JJ Club's partnerships with luxury brands?

We now have over 120 luxury likeminded brand partners in our digital club for all our members to benefit from - every day. Some of our most popular perks and benefits so far are from within our food & drink, parenting & pets, wellness & beauty and travel & culture pillars - partners such as Roarsome, Chez Bruce, Barracudas & Sports Fusion, Champagnes & Chateaux, Turquoise Holidays, Calder & Co and Fair Oak Farm. Our events calendar is also proving popular with members enjoying Reformer Pilates, personal training with Oliver Black, and Millie & Maisie soft play and cooking classes.

### How do you see The JJ Club evolving once the flagship physical site opens, and what additional benefits will it offer to members?

The JJ Club physical club will be a luxurious, family members club for the whole family to work, rest & play. We will ensure spaces for the kids to be entertained (& supervised), as much as spaces for adults to enjoy, work, stay fit and relax, and spaces for families to hang out together too. We're planning a pool and gym, large co-working space, screening room, and 2 distinct areas for tots, tweens and teens, alongside 2 restaurants. The vision is to open the first flagship site amongst my own community (I have lived in SW London all my life) and then look to other affluent London villages and beyond that also needs a space and club like this locally to make a difference.

PHOTO:*Jacqueline Iversen, Co-Founder and Chief Clinical Officer of Sen-Jam Pharmaceutical, leading the charge in innovative and proactive pain management solutions.*

# Wisdom from a Wellness Innovator JACQUELINE IVERSEN

## *Empowering Future Pharmacists and Entrepreneurs*

*Jacqueline Iversen discusses Sen-Jam Pharmaceutical's innovative approach to pain management, emphasizing proactive solutions, accessibility, and the importance of creativity and perseverance in healthcare.*

When it comes to innovation in pain management and wellness, few names resonate as strongly as Jacqueline Iversen. As the Co-Founder and Chief Clinical Officer of Sen-Jam Pharmaceutical, Jackie has dedicated her career to rethinking the traditional paradigms of the pharmaceutical industry. Her extensive background in pharmacokinetics and pain management, combined with her unwavering commitment to improving patient outcomes, has positioned her as a visionary in the field. With over two decades of scientific contributions, including more than 20 published papers, Jackie is not only a leader in clinical research but also a passionate advocate for proactive and preventive healthcare solutions.

Jackie's journey began with a vision during her research fellowship at Memorial Sloan Kettering, where she recognized the need for a shift from reactive to proactive pain management strategies. Her expertise as a hospital pharmacist, coupled with her deep understanding of the challenges faced by patients, inspired her to co-found Sen-Jam Pharmaceutical alongside her husband, Jim, a logistics and efficiency expert. Together, they have cultivated a unique approach to drug development, focusing on low-cost, repurposed therapeutics that aim to reduce healthcare expenditures while expanding access to underserved populations.

In this exclusive interview for Entrepreneur Prime Magazine, Jackie shares her insights on the inspiration behind Sen-Jam Pharmaceutical, the personal experiences that fuel her determination to address inflammation, pain, and addiction, and the innovative strategies her company employs to navigate the complexities of the pharmaceutical industry. She also provides valuable advice for aspiring pharmacists and entrepreneurs, emphasizing the importance of creativity, perseverance, and data-driven decision-making in driving meaningful change.

Join us as we delve into the mind of a true wellness innovator and explore the future of pain management and global health through the eyes of Jacqueline Iversen.

### How did you and your husband Jim come up with the idea to start Sen-Jam Pharmaceutical?

I founded Sen-Jam Pharmaceutical because I had a vision around improving our current standard of pain management which stemmed

*Jacqueline Iversen is a pioneering force in clinical pain management and pharmaceutical innovation, dedicated to transforming patient care and advancing wellness.*

from my research fellowship at Memorial Sloan Kettering in New York City. It was during that time, decades ago, that I first became fascinated by how the medical community treated pain well after the fact or reactively instead of considering means of preventing or mitigating it proactively. I am a hospital pharmacist who loves science and sees thousands of people yearly who continue to struggle with ailments, despite the plethora of medications currently available. I have always wanted to improve outcomes with evidence based ideas that challenge the status quo. As for my husband; he's a brilliant business mind rooted deeply in logistics and efficiency. Bringing that sharp solutions-orientation to the infamously old-school pharma industry has been a true competitive advantage to our success. Rethinking the industry paradigm, with Jim at the helm as CEO and I as Chief Clinical Officer, we believed it would result in new, more innovative products reaching patients in need. And we both wanted that challenge.

### What personal experiences have shaped your determination to create solutions for inflammation, pain, and addiction?

As a pharmacist, but more so, as a human, seeing the devastation and suffering brought onto individuals and their families, plaguing our society and the world by unethical pharmaceutical business practices, utilizing addictive drugs, makes me so angry, that I have felt a personal duty to use my knowledge to help out where I can. I realized, had alternative pharmaceutical products been developed just before Oxycontin, we could have reduced the risk and devastation of widespread opioid addiction and dependence. I believe that drug development has the potential to change prescribing and drug policy, by educating everyone, and I wanted to share my knowledge this way. An idea that could be distributed to many. That's where my research began, treating pain with a non-opioid agent that also reduces the harmful effects of opioids. And along the way, I've additionally discovered new treatments to reduce inflammation, and safely modulate the immune system, which coincidentally, is intimately tied to pain and addiction.

### What challenges have you faced in developing low-cost therapeutics for underserved populations, and how have you overcome them?

The majority of drugs, over 50% each year that obtain FDA approval, are repurposed, low-cost therapeutics that could reduce healthcare expenditure - particularly in the United States, but elsewhere as well - and expand access to all populations. And the majority of companies develop drugs in that repurposed space; which makes it very crowded. Yet, the larger investors focus on what we would consider "designer drugs" which are where larger pharma companies reside. That risk to reward benefit is extremely high. This designer investment model makes the length of time to develop a drug longer, for both the pharmaceutical company and the patient. Which is where Sen-Jam sees the opportunity of rapidly and at low cost, developing innovative products that can challenge the larger pharmaceutical company inventions by targeting the same unique mechanism of action, but with an already available, known to be safe, drug. So being nimble, is our secret sauce, as we leverage new technology (i.e. artificial intelligence, digital clinical trials, companion diagnostics, collaborative partnerships, etc.) to achieve our goals of bringing new and superior solutions to patients as fast as possible.

### How do you envision the future of Sen-Jam Pharmaceutical in terms of its impact on global health?

Sen-Jam is on a mission to extend healthy aging by safely modulating our immune system. The immune system is just now, being understood and mapped, into a vast web of differentiated cells and mediators that influence our health for a lifetime. Sen-Jam's mission is to support an individual's immune system, by first ensuring propering monitoring, and measuring of the immune system's role in health and disease. And secondly, or more deliberately, treating inflammation further upstream proactively (meaning before tissue damage and disease have taken root) than current therapeutics do. It's currently believed that with overuse, our immune system can become fragile, and slow, leading to diseases that require very potent, immunosuppressive treatments (i.e. costly "designer drugs" for Inflammatory bowel disease, arthritis, cancer, etc). By targeting inflammation using a broad-spectrum anti-inflammatory without damaging the immune system more, Sen-Jam is able to proactively change the course of inflammation for more than half the world. And inflammation comes in several forms: acute, chronic, autoimmune, and low grade chronic inflammation. We believe we can protect the immune system by preventing and reducing the initial cascade of inflammation that occurs, whether from our environment (diet, stress, allergies, substances of abuse, etc) or from disease (cardiometabolic, autoimmune or cancer).

### What advice would you give to aspiring pharmacists and entrepreneurs looking to make a difference in the pharmaceutical industry?

I believe that history repeats itself, and all the large pharmaceutical companies were initially started by a pharmacist, with an idea. And entrepreneurs are filled with new ideas infused with creativity. I believe that is where it begins, and then you start walking that path and learning how to do it your unique way. The industry is massive, and there are a lot of opportunities with some hard work. So your passion has to be your calling. Don't be afraid to bring a fresh mind to these large entrenched problems. In fact, we believe Einstein had it right when he said "you cannot solve a problem with the same consciousness that created it." Trust your instincts when something seems off to you and follow the data fiercely. The industry needs creative problem solvers like you so go out there and explore what's possible. Expect to face adversity, especially where money is holding the power in the room, but have conviction in your beliefs (and your data!) and always do your best.

### Can you provide more details about Sen-Jam Pharmaceutical's recent partnership with a pharmaceutical manufacturer, Manufacturing & Controls (CMC), of your anti-inflammatory injectable, and how this collaboration will impact your product development and distribution?

Our partnership with KVK-Tech is a massive accelerant to our drug development activities. By working closely and early with our incredibly capable colleagues at this world-class manufacturing and controls organization, we are able to produce the highest quality product in the most efficient means possible. KVK and Sen-Jam forged an initial partnership around our oral mast cell modulator and recently entered a third drug development project together with the plans of developing the first mast cell modulating injectable for hospital use. We believe this product offers a much needed tool for physicians to transform care in that setting.

“
True innovation
should never
compromise
integrity.”
– Pascale Rothman

# PASCALE ROTHMAN

# The Visionary Behind More. Longevity & Wellbeing

By Lyra Green

In an era where wellness has become a buzzword, Pascale Rothman, the visionary Founder and CEO of More. Longevity & Wellbeing, stands at the forefront of a transformative movement. With a commitment to integrity, transparency, and community engagement, Rothman is redefining what it means to pursue health and well-being. In this exclusive feature with Beauty Prime magazine, she shares her insights on fostering a culture of innovation, addressing industry challenges, and the strategic vision that will guide More. Longevity & Wellbeing into the future. As the wellness landscape continues to evolve, Rothman's approach offers a refreshing perspective that prioritizes substance over trends, aiming to empower consumers to make informed choices for lasting health.

### FOSTERING A CULTURE OF WELLNESS

At More. Longevity & Wellbeing, the commitment to fostering a culture of wellness is integral to operations. The company's ethos revolves around empowering its team members to share their expertise, creating an environment where everyone feels valued for their contributions. This foundation of mutual trust enhances job satisfaction, drives creativity, and encourages a sense of community. Rothman emphasizes that true innovation should never compromise integrity, a guiding principle that shapes the product development process. By prioritizing ethical practices and rigorous quality control, More. Longevity & Wellbeing ensures that its offerings consistently exceed consumer expectations.

*Pascale Rothman redefines wellness with More. Longevity & Wellbeing, prioritizing integrity, transparency, and innovation. Her approach challenges industry norms while fostering community-driven, sustainable health solutions for lasting impact on consumers' lives.*

### EMBRACING CHALLENGES AS OPPORTUNITIES

The wellness industry is currently facing significant challenges, particularly regarding product integrity. Many companies cut costs by providing ineffective dosages of ingredients, undermining product quality. Rothman views this as an opportunity to elevate industry standards. More. Longevity & Wellbeing is committed to science and will not compromise on the essential elements of its products. The belief that wellness should be both achievable and a pleasurable experience sets the company apart in a highly saturated marketplace. By creating potent and palatable products, More. Longevity & Wellbeing enhances the consumer experience and promotes a genuine appreciation for nutrition. The organization is dedicated to the wellness journey, ensuring that its blends provide robust health advantages.

## Empowering Health Through Integrity And Innovation

### A VISION FOR LASTING HEALTH

Rothman's inspiration for leading More. Longevity & Wellbeing stems from a critical gap she identified in the wellness industry: the need for a brand that focuses on lasting health rather than fleeting fads. Many products promise quick fixes but overlook the principles of effective wellness. More. Longevity & Wellbeing advocates for a data-driven approach that emphasizes consistency, mindfulness, and the use of high-quality ingredients. The mission is to restore integrity and transparency in the Natural Products Industry, empowering consumers to make informed choices that enhance their wellness. By raising industry standards, the company seeks to deepen the connection between consumers and their health, reshaping the wellness landscape by prioritizing substance and efficacy.

### STRATEGIC VISION FOR THE FUTURE

Looking ahead, Rothman has a well-defined strategic vision for More. Longevity & Wellbeing over the next five years. The organization aims to maintain its leadership position within the wellness industry by prioritizing transparency, efficacy, and quality. As the industry undergoes continual evolution, the company remains committed to its foundational principles, ensuring that its products are not only effective but also seamlessly integrated into daily routines. Plans for global expansion are underway, alongside a focus on innovation. Rothman envisions developing new products that harmoniously combine natural potency with indulgent flavors—an aspect frequently neglected in the wellness sector.

### INNOVATION AT THE CORE

Innovation is at the heart of More. Longevity & Wellbeing's product offerings. The company recognizes the demand for efficacious supplements, understanding that the success of such products relies on the quality, dosage, and synergy between the featured ingredients. The effectiveness of supplements begins with high-quality raw materials, and bioavailable compounds enhance absorption, making them more effective. Ingredients supported by scientific research are crucial for achieving desired outcomes, and the team is in tune with the latest trends and developments within the natural space.

### MEASURING COMMUNITY IMPACT

Measuring impact on community health and wellness is another priority for More. Longevity & Wellbeing. The organization quantitatively assesses its success through the compelling narratives and transformative experiences shared by its community members. These individual accounts serve as evidence of the profound impact that the products provide. More. Longevity & Wellbeing prioritizes relationship-building over transactional sales. As the organization grows, there is a strategic intent to intensify these connections through direct community engagement and the establishment of educational platforms. By equipping consumers with knowledge and tools, the company aims to empower individuals who seek wellness.

### A LASTING IMPACT

In a world where wellness trends often come and go, Pascale Rothman and More. Longevity & Wellbeing are committed to creating a lasting impact. By focusing on integrity, transparency, and community engagement, they are not just selling products; they are fostering a movement towards genuine well-being. As the wellness landscape continues to evolve, Rothman's vision and leadership will undoubtedly play a pivotal role in shaping the future of health and wellness for consumers everywhere.

Neil Leonard, captured in his creative element, a trailblazing composer and artist whose work bridges the worlds of sound, technology, and culture.

# NEIL LEONARD

# Blends Music, Technology, and Culture to Create Captivating Interdisciplinary Art

By Hazel Ivy

Neil Leonard stands as a truly visionary figure whose expansive oeuvre bridges the realms of sound, sight, and technology. As a composer, saxophonist, and transdisciplinary artist, his innovative works transcend traditional boundaries, creating immersive experiences that invite audiences into new dimensions of artistic exploration. From performances at iconic venues like Carnegie Hall to groundbreaking installations at the Venice Biennale and Tate Modern, Leonard's artistry exemplifies both technical mastery and emotional resonance. His ability to harmonize live electronics, multichannel audio, and traditional music forms with visual and spatial elements speaks to his boundless creativity and enduring impact on contemporary art. Furthermore, Leonard's commitment to fostering interdisciplinary collaboration as the founding Artistic Director of Berklee Interdisciplinary Arts Institute underscores his dedication to shaping the next generation of boundary-defying artists.

In this issue of *Mosaci Digest*, we delve into the mind of Neil Leonard, exploring his global collaborations, cutting-edge technological approaches, and his lifelong dialogue with the worlds of music and visual art. Through an exclusive interview, Leonard shares insights into his creative process, recounts transformative experiences from his international projects, and reflects on the profound power of listening as both an artistic and communal act. His story is one of unyielding curiosity, innovation, and an unshakable belief in the symbiosis of diverse art forms and cultures.

*Neil Leonard's groundbreaking artistry redefines boundaries, seamlessly weaving music, technology, and culture into dynamic, thought-provoking interdisciplinary masterpieces.*

**Your career spans a wide range of disciplines, from music composition to multimedia perfor-mance. How do you approach blending these different forms of art in your work?**

I'm fascinated by the interplay between visual art, sound, and music. From a young age, I ex-plored painting, drawing, printmaking, and animation. After formal music training in jazz saxo-phone at the New England Conservatory, I worked at the Massachusetts College of Art, where I began collaborating with visual artists in film, video, performance, and installation. One early interdisciplinary project was creating sound and music for Tony Oursler's work, featured in the Whitney Biennial.

A recent example of my interdisciplinary approach is Frequências Futurais, developed during a 2023 residency at the Sacatar Institute in Brazil. While on the Island of Itaparica, I immersed myself in the environment—recording local sounds, gathering residents' spoken histories, and creating daily electronic compositions. The result was a sound, video, and sculptural installa-tion, exhibited at Galleria Solar Ferrão in Salvador de Bahia, and later presented at IRCAM in Paris and Experimental Loop in NYC in 2024.

*Neil Leonard discusses his global collaborations, blending visual art, sound, and technology, alongside his process for creating immersive installations, fostering interdisciplinary education, and exploring the transformative power of listening across cultures.*

**Having collaborated with artists across the globe, including in places like Cuba, Israel, and Ja-pan, how have these international experiences influenced your creative process?**

Collaborating with artists across the globe has shown me how essential it is to pay attention to the voices of my collaborators and their communities to enrich our work together. My experi-ence with Cuban artists, in particular, has highlighted how listening can build trust across cul-tural differences.

Lately, I've been reflecting on the importance of collaborative listening. I've applied this ap-proach in Matanzas Sound Map, which will be exhibited at Tate Modern in 2025. This installa-tion invites the audience to embark on a listening journey that began in Cuba, where I collabo-rated with musicians, biologists, street criers, and others to explore how people uniquely hear their surroundings. From folkloric music to the sounds of dawn in the Ciénaga de Zapata bio-sphere, the project captures the rich sonic landscape of the Matanzas province. The piece was created in collaboration with artist Maria Magdalena Campos-Pons.

**Many of your performances incorporate live electronics and multichannel audio. What drives your interest in integrating technology with traditional music forms?**

I am always curious about exploring new artistic possibilities. Each era has its own technologi-cal innovations. Centuries ago the concept of the musical scale was a new technology. The sax-ophone itself has only been popular for the past one hundred years. The synthesizer became widely used in my lifetime. In the 1980s I began creating software that responded to my per-formance. My album Timeaus (2001) features original compositions for saxophone and soft-ware in which I used musical prompts for machine generated response in realtime. This work predates the widespread use of AI by thirty years.

**You've worked with notable artists like Tony Oursler and Fujiko Nakaya, and showcased your installations at prestigious venues like MoMA and Tate Modern. Can you share what goes into creating large-scale interdisciplinary collaborations?**

Large-scale interdisciplinary collaborations begin with active listening—listening to collabora-tors to understand their vision, to the unique acoustic elements of the space, and to develop a shared aesthetic. This practice has shaped my creative process across international projects. One notable example is my collaboration with Fujiko Nakaya. After attending my concert Sound-ing the Cloud at the Institute of Contemporary Art in Boston, she invited me to compose for her installation Fog x Ruins in Franklin Park. The installation—a 30 x 12-meter structure with 900 mist nozzles—was set in a historic stone ruin where Duke Ellington once held free concerts. My composition blended with Fujiko's fog, inviting the audience into a space where they could no-tice the subtle shifts in wind, light, and mist. Fujiko later told me, "It was with your music that I discovered sound gave form to fog or a/form to no/form."

**As the founding Artistic Director of the Berklee Interdisciplinary Arts Institute, how do you fos-ter an environment that encourages students to explore cross-disciplinary art forms?**

My goal is to teach students the practice of collaborating with artists from diverse disciplines. I encourage them to explore their own art while connecting with different cultures. I invite prac-ticing artists and curators working in interdisciplinary spaces to share their work and critique students' projects. We also collaborate with schools like Harvard, MIT, and the Shanghai Thea-ter Academy.

**Your compositions and installations have been featured in iconic spaces like Carnegie Hall and the Venice Biennale. How do you tailor your work for such diverse venues and audiences?**

The site of a piece shapes its unique listening context. At the Venice Biennale, I drew on the spatial experiments of composers like Giovanni Gabrieli at San Marco, positioning 18 loud-speakers in the National Museum of Archaeology for an antiphonal experience, where street vendor voices, electronic sounds, and conversations surrounded visitors, blending with the bells of the Campanile.

In contrast, when composing Totems for Don Byron at Carnegie Hall, I left space for the audi-ence to appreciate the hall's acoustics. Each work is crafted for its venue, and its context doesn't transfer easily

Reader's House
Italian Roots, Canadian Stories
BARBARA AVON
Telling Stories That Haunt, Heal and Inspire Across Genres
INTERVIEW
Voices of Literary Excellence
Insights from Today's Celebrated Authors
David Gordon
Joseph Schwartz
Linnea Tanner
A.D. Vancise
Catalina Dubois
A.Cristibor
Colin Van Dongen
Mia Van Dongen
Budd Titlow
C.R. Fabis
Mark Gorkin
Ruth Fein
Shaun Goldsmith
Sherry Argov
Peter Ralston
Gwen McPhail
EDITOR'S CHOICE
Best Books to Dive Into

Subscribe Now!

**YES!** I would like a subscription to

☐ Current Issue for ☐ Includes Shipping and Handling

☐ One-Year Subscription ( _____ Issues) for

☐ Two-Year Subscription ( _____ Issues) for

☐ I am a renewing a current subscription ☐ I am a new subscriber

Name: ______________________ Phone: ______________

Shipping Address: ______________________

Billing Address: ______________________

Email: ______________________

☐ Yes, I would like to receive updates, newsletters and special offers

☐ No, I would NOT like to receive updates, newsletters and special offers

**Payment Type:** ☐ Cash ☐ Check

Please mail this form to:

**Magazine Name:** *Reader's House* by Newyox 200 Suite, 134-146 Curtain Road EC2A 3AR London readershouse.co.uk

www.ingramcontent.com/pod-product-compliance
Lightning Source LLC
Chambersburg PA
CBHW041206100726
47911CB00016B/875
*9781642264340*